UNIVERSITY OF CAMBRIDGE

MUSEUM OF ZOOLOGY
UNIVERSITY OF CAMBRIDGE

The ANIMAL QUEENDOM

Catherine Blackledge

Kasia Bogdańska

nosy crow

For my family:
Willow, Maisie and Steve,
and in memory of
my mum and dad.

C.B.

To my family:
Pola, Maja and Michał and
to my mother and mother-in-law.

K.B.

With special thanks to Dr Rosalyn Wade
of the University Museum of Zoology, Cambridge,
for her contribution and advice.

First published 2026 by Nosy Crow Ltd
Wheat Wharf, 27a Shad Thames
London, SE1 2XZ, UK

Nosy Crow Eireann Ltd
Fieldfisher Ireland LLP
45 Mespil Road, Dublin 4,
Dublin, D04 W2F1, Ireland

www.nosycrow.com

ISBN 978 1 80513 545 6

Published by Nosy Crow in collaboration with the University of Cambridge.

A CIP catalogue record for this book is available from the British Library.

Printed in Italy following rigorous ethical sourcing standards.

1 3 5 7 9 8 6 4 2

Daring and dangerous

Colourful critters

Contents

Clever communicators

Fearless leaders

Awesomely adaptable

Sensational senses

Powerful parents

Conclusion

Introduction

Welcome to the animal queendom! This book is a celebration of nature's fantastic, fearless female animals, some of whom are the deadliest and most powerful on Earth. Across these pages, you'll unearth astonishing facts about familiar species and discover jaw-dropping creatures you've never even heard of!

It's often the impressive female of a species whose fierce behaviours or unusual appearance deserve attention. Did you know that if you're stung by a bee, wasp or ant, or are bitten by a mosquito, your attacker is a female? Only females are equipped with the weaponry needed to sting or drink blood!

Not only are most female animals bigger and stronger than males of the same species, but several hold world records for size and speed. Look out for these awesome female record breakers throughout this book, including the most massive creature to have ever existed (pages 54-55).

Our planet has many more female animals living on it than male animals because some species give birth to many more females than males. Some female animals are so incredible that they can create babies all by themselves, while others only ever have female babies – males of their species have never been found. We really do live in an animal queendom!

Their unique biology means that females and males of the same species can look and act completely differently. The two sexes exist because two different special cells called 'gametes' – one from a female and one from a male – are usually (but not always!) required to make a baby animal.

Female animals are defined as the sex with the body plan to make large gametes (eggs). Male animals are defined as the sex with the body plan to produce small gametes (sperm).

Shockingly, it's only in the last 100 years that we've begun to appreciate how extraordinary female animals are. For a long time, most wildlife experts were men who ignored female animals or came to incorrect conclusions about what they are capable of. Some presumed that women were not competitive or aggressive, and so assumed female animals couldn't be either. They were wrong on all counts!

Opinions only began to change when increasing numbers of women got the opportunity to study animals. They noticed the striking features and startling abilities of female animals, placing female wildlife in the scientific spotlight for the very first time and inspiring others to investigate the remarkable queendom we live in (see pages 76-77 for more on this).

Within this book, you'll meet not only the world's fastest, heaviest and largest animals, but also crafty colour-changing creatures, deeply devoted mums and even surprisingly murderous mammals. It's time to forget everything you think you know about female animals, so get ready to dive headfirst into the wonders of the animal queendom!

Swift-striking snakes

Reticulated python

LONGEST SNAKE ON EARTH

With jaws that can open extraordinarily wide to swallow her prey whole, the female reticulated python is strong, stealthy and extremely deadly. Even humans are on her menu!

Massive meals

Like most snake species, female reticulated pythons are more massive than males. Females can be almost double the male's length and four times their weight!

A fearless female can hunt bulkier and more dangerous prey, while males stick to snacking on smaller animals like rats. Antelope and wild boar are usually her meal of choice, but occasionally humans are up for grabs as well. You really don't want to meet her when she's hungry!

Bigger, stronger and hungrier – females are much more dangerous than males.

Reticulated pythons swallow their prey whole.

RECORD BREAKER

The female reticulated python is the world's longest snake! Females up to 10 metres long have been recorded in the wild (that's as long as six human adults laid head to toe on the ground).

Female *Male*

SIZE COMPARISON

A baby snake exits its egg.

EXCELLENT EGGS

Being bigger allows female reticulated pythons to have more and larger babies than other snakes, giving these babies a better chance of surviving. Their eggs are almost twice the size of a chicken's egg! Mothers typically lay around 40 large white oval eggs but can have clutches of over 100 eggs.

Lying in wait

Reticulated pythons kill by lying in wait in the rainforest and woodlands of Southeast Asia, camouflaged by the net-like (reticulated) pattern running the length of their body. A female strikes quickly, biting with her sharp, backwards-pointing teeth to secure her prey and then almost instantly wrapping her muscular coils around her victim. She squeezes so tightly that her prey's heart stops beating or they suffocate. It's very tough to make an escape!

Meerkats on a mission

Meerkats live in African deserts, in family mobs of up to 50 animals. A large and aggressive female, the alpha, controls life in the group and is mum to most young meerkats in the pack.

The alpha's main mission in life is to have as many babies as possible, but doing this in a harsh desert environment is difficult. To succeed, she must make all other mob members help care for her babies and cannot allow them to have any young of their own. She needs to use violence to achieve her goal!

An alpha can force females to leave her mob.

Banished from the burrow

If other female meerkats become pregnant, they are forced to leave the group's underground home and fend for themselves in the dangerous desert. If any do give birth in the burrow, the alpha meerkat shows no mercy, killing and eating the pups before banishing the mother.

CRUEL FOR A REASON

The alpha's actions may be cruel, but being ruthless means she keeps her young safe. A female alpha can have more than 80 pups during her lifetime!

Rules for returning

During pregnancy, the alpha female meerkat becomes increasingly aggressive, scratching, biting and snatching food from lower-status females to keep them in their place. After the alpha has given birth, banished female group members are allowed to return home – but only if they agree to look after her babies!

Alphas on the attack

Meerkat

This female creature looks cute, but her behaviour is anything but! The alpha female meerkat is the queen of mean and will stop at nothing to get her own way. She bullies and attacks her sisters and daughters and even eats her grandchildren! This small, furry female is possibly the most murderous mammal on Earth.

Alpha females show no mercy to other meerkats, even babies.

Murderous male-eaters

Black widow spider

Female black widow spiders have a terrifying reputation – and it's a well-deserved one! Found across most of North America, females of the species are far more deadly and frightening than males.

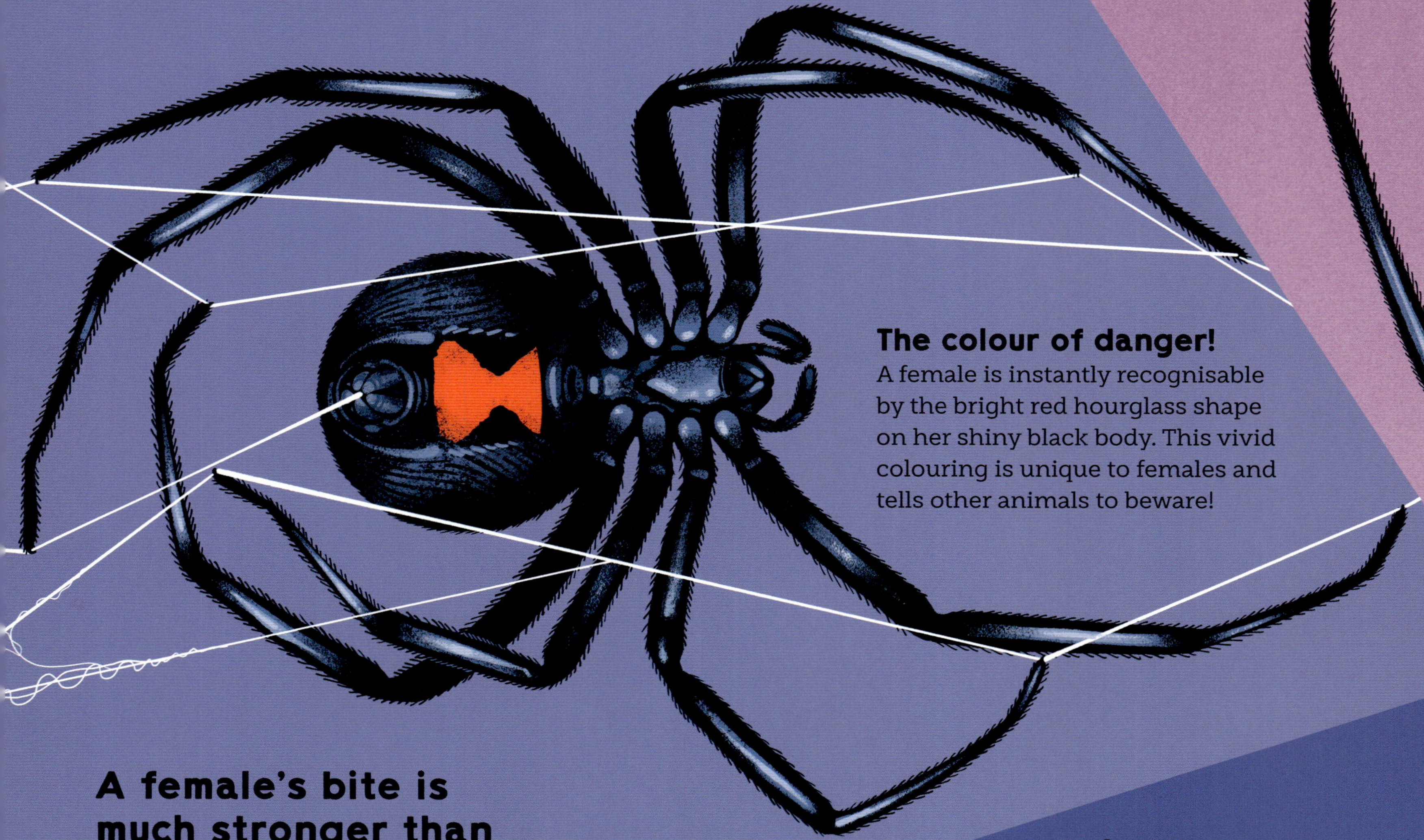

The colour of danger!

A female is instantly recognisable by the bright red hourglass shape on her shiny black body. This vivid colouring is unique to females and tells other animals to beware!

A female's bite is much stronger than a male's – it's powerful enough to puncture human skin!

A RUTHLESS PARTNER

She's called the black widow because of her murderous habit of sometimes eating her male partner after mating (at 3.5 centimetres, she's at least twice the size of him!).

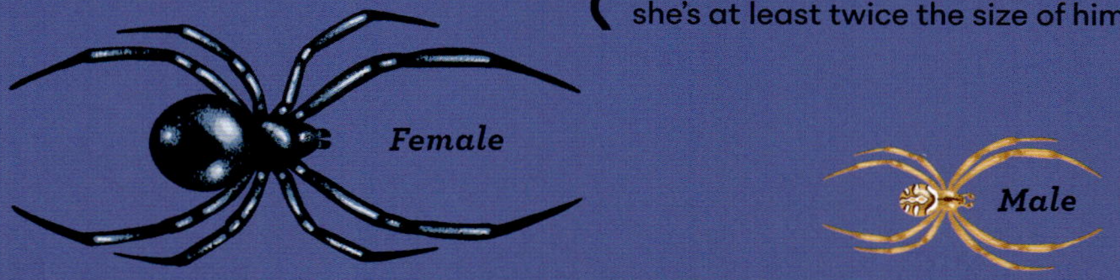

SIZE COMPARISON

Fang-tastic features

If provoked, she's one of the few spiders who will bite humans. She has large venom glands, powerful biting muscles and long hollow fangs pointed enough to puncture human skin (the male's bite is too weak for this).

She injects her venom through her sharp teeth – quickly paralysing and killing her victim. While she often preys on large mice, lizards, birds and insects, human bites are rarely fatal.

Super-strong silk

A female black widow has a special weapon – her spider silk. She traps, injects and devours smaller prey in the strands of her amazing web. It's as tough as Kevlar, a material which can stop bullets!

Females (but not males) also have a special skill called 'silk-flicking', which allows them to battle larger animals. By shooting extra-sticky silk from spinnerets on her abdomen, a female black widow can immobilise a victim, covering it in silk before she moves in for the kill. Approach this spider at your peril!

Bone-crushing killers

Spotted hyena

Female spotted hyenas are bold, brawny and ferocious predators. From their very first days on the African plains, they fight more viciously and frequently than male pups. Thanks to their greater size, strength and drive to be top dog, all females are superior to males and an alpha female leads the clan.

Back off!

An alpha female commands a clan of up to 130 hyenas, leading charges against rivals trying to take over her territory and snatch her group's prey. Clan wars are violent and hyenas can be injured and killed, but the alpha female fiercely attacks intruders in order to keep control of her queendom.

Hyenas can crush bones with their powerful jaws!

Feeding frenzies

Although they have a reputation as scavengers, hyenas are strong hunters. Sharp teeth and bone-cracking jaws mean hyenas are able to bring down prey such as zebra and wildebeest up to three times their weight. Mealtimes are highly competitive feeding frenzies: a whole carcass can be devoured, bones included, within 30 minutes!

Violent fights often break out, but females don't back down from danger. Their rank means they eat first, while males must wait their turn – or risk being attacked!

Menacing mums

Female spotted hyenas are super strong and dangerous because they need to secure food during mealtime scrums. When pregnant and breastfeeding, mothers require extra food for energy. Later, when her pup begins to eat meat, a mum will physically force rivals to back off during mealtimes so her slower, smaller pup can feed safely. If she can't do this, her pup will starve – so she needs to be a big, bad, dangerous mother!

These fierce females won't back down from a fight, and will do what it takes to become top dog.

Super-powerful predators

Great white shark

With multiple rows of jagged, razor-sharp teeth, great white sharks are a terrifying sight. All great whites are fearsome predators, but it's the more massive females who are typically the deadliest hunters.

Out of nowhere

Imagine being a seal, alone in the ocean. One second, you're swimming along. The next, a gaping jaw clamps shut around you as its owner rockets out of the water. Less than a minute later, your life is over. Mega shark strikes are fast, furious and efficient – despite their large size, great whites can reach speeds of up to 40 kilometres per hour when hunting seals, fish and dolphins.

RECORD BREAKER

Female great whites are significantly bigger than males. Growing up to six metres in length, they are the planet's largest living carnivorous fish!

Who's the boss?

Great whites mostly live and hunt alone in the ocean but when two sharks do meet, they literally size each other up to see who's boss. The biggest shark is usually the female, so she wins! As well as expertly pursuing their own prey, females use their elevated status in shark society to cheekily snatch prey caught by smaller, lower-ranking male sharks.

These deadly hunters use their size to show males not to mess with them.

UNDER ATTACK?
Shark attacks on surfing and swimming humans are very rare, thankfully, but do happen every year, in particular off the coast of Australia and the United States of America.

Two great white shark pups swim together.

A big reputation

Females carry and give birth to around 10 hefty pups at one time; each weighs roughly the same as an 11-year-old child (about 35 kilograms) and is around 1.5 metres long! Female great white sharks must be larger and deadlier than males in order to keep growing shark pups safe inside their bodies. Their size and skillset also help strengthen their reputation as one of the most frightening fish on Earth.

RECORD BREAKER
Frightful, a particularly speedy female, was recorded diving at 389 kilometres per hour during an experiment!

Spectacular strikes

A female reaches her top speeds during her steep dive for prey (called a 'stoop'). Rising high above her victim and tucking in her wings, she tilts her flight path to almost vertical and plummets earthwards – a furious, feathered missile ready to strike and stun her prey with a massive mid-air blow.

Queen of the chase

These birds are built for breakneck speed. While in a dive, a falcon holds her body in a teardrop shape, which reduces how much the wind slows her down. Sweptback, lightweight wings and slim, stiff feathers help with this too. Finally, a female's breastbone offers a large area for her enhanced flight muscles to attach to, giving her the crucial power to withstand the extreme wind force encountered during fast-moving flight. She's the undisputed queen of the high-speed chase!

A female feeds her chicks with fresh prey.

Furiously fast falcons

Peregrine falcon

FASTEST ANIMAL ON EARTH

The winner of the ultimate animal race, the female peregrine falcon is the fastest bird in the world and the fastest animal on the planet. Female falcons' extra size and strength make them record-breaking super-speedsters and allow them to be even more daring hunters than their male counterparts.

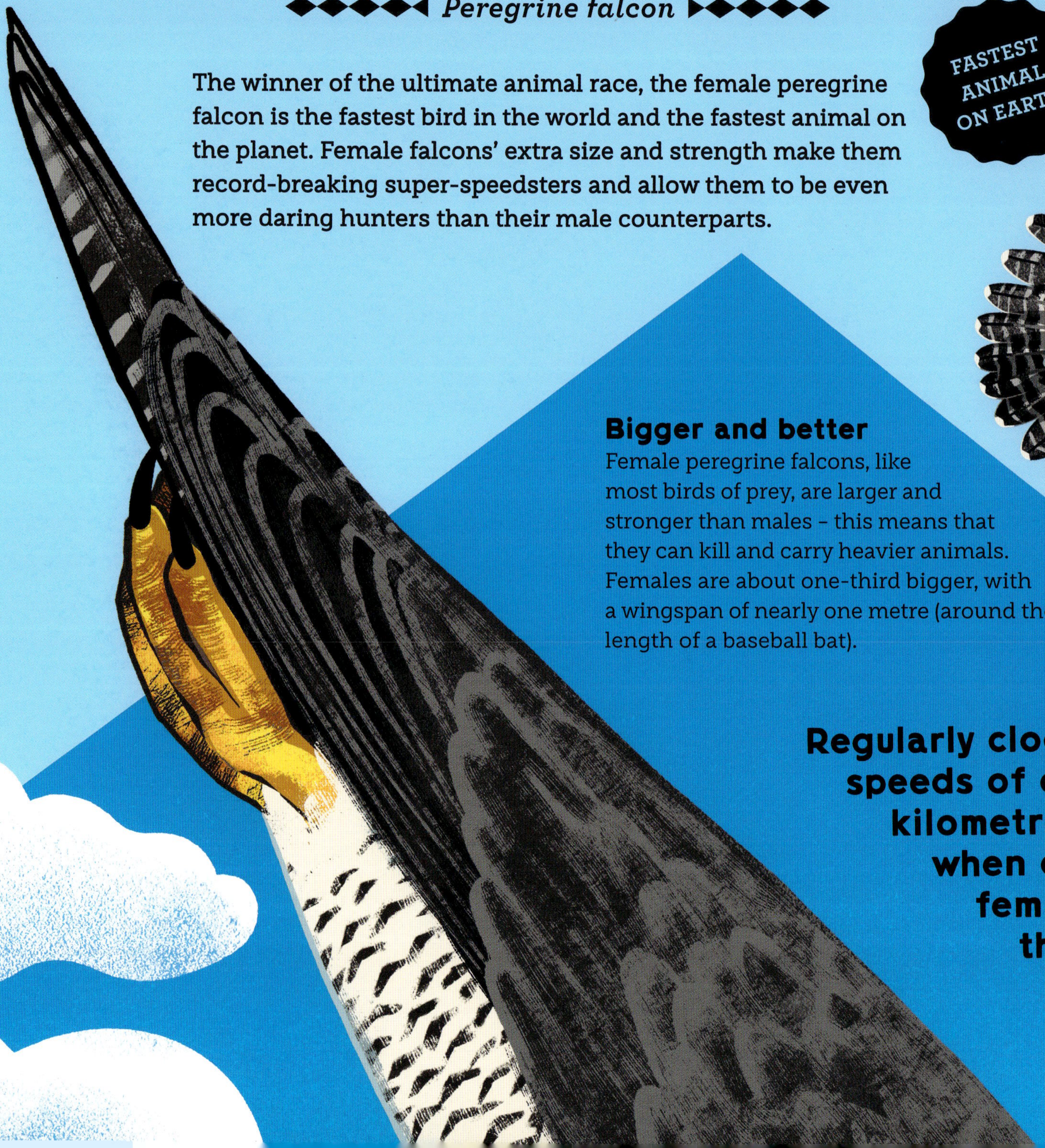

Bigger and better

Female peregrine falcons, like most birds of prey, are larger and stronger than males – this means that they can kill and carry heavier animals. Females are about one-third bigger, with a wingspan of nearly one metre (around the length of a baseball bat).

Regularly clocking speeds of over 320 kilometres per hour when diving for prey, females are faster than a Formula 1 car!

Spectacular sea creatures

Blanket octopus

With her shimmering multi-coloured cape billowing behind her, the female blanket octopus looks like a magnificent superheroine of the deep. Her rainbow cloak is key to not only her survival but also her very large family's!

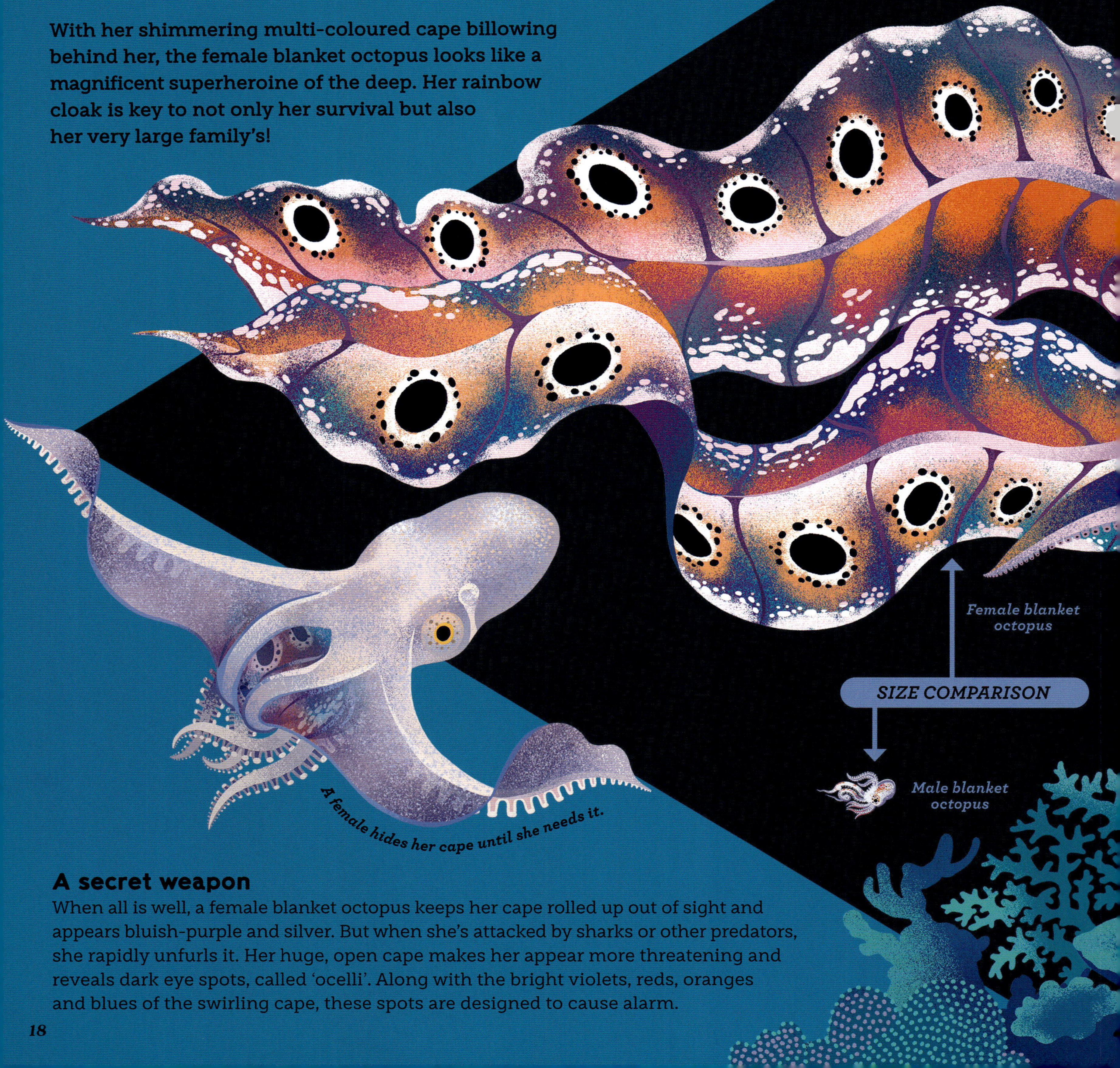

A secret weapon

When all is well, a female blanket octopus keeps her cape rolled up out of sight and appears bluish-purple and silver. But when she's attacked by sharks or other predators, she rapidly unfurls it. Her huge, open cape makes her appear more threatening and reveals dark eye spots, called 'ocelli'. Along with the bright violets, reds, oranges and blues of the swirling cape, these spots are designed to cause alarm.

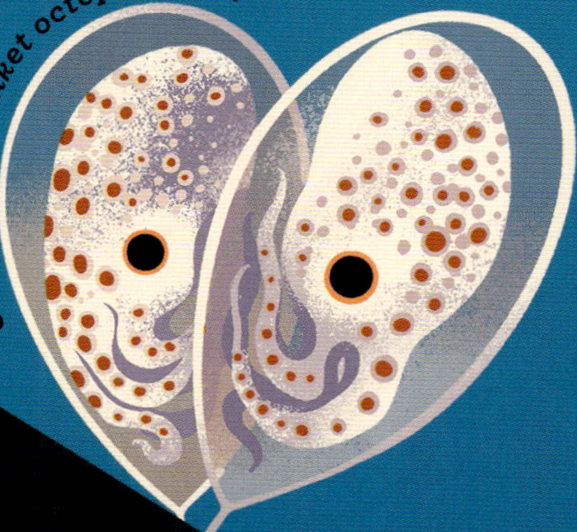

Close-up of blanket octopus eggs.

Giants of the deep

A female blanket octopus swims freely in her tropical home, rather than hiding for safety. She must guard and carry 150,000 small, soft eggs, so she has to be able to defend herself! Her responsibilities mean she is very different to her male partner: she's at least 100 times longer and 40,000 times heavier. Males don't have a cape and are the size of a walnut, or one of the female's eyes!

SWITCHING SHADES

A female blanket octopus' cape can change colour because it contains special cells called 'chromatophores'. When these cells expand or shrink, they cause her skin to shift from one shade to another.

Defensive decoy

Females have another clever trick up their sleeves. When in danger, she can use her cape as a decoy, leaving it behind to grab her enemy's attention while she and her eggs make a quick getaway!

With swirling colours and menacing eye spots, a female's cape scares off predators and protects her family.

A female must keep 150,000 eggs safe.

Striking shade-shifters

Flower crab spider

Imagine being able to change your entire body colour to match your background! It's an impressive party trick, and one which female flower crab spiders perform regularly. Experts at surprising their prey, females switch between shades of yellow, cream and white to match the flowers they are hunting on. Why female flower crab spiders have this unusual colour-swapping ability, and why the smaller, darker males don't, is an unsolved mystery.

A flower crab spider can match the shade of the flower she is hunting on.

Only females of this species can change colour – easily shifting between different shades while males remain the same.

Flower crab spiders hunt flies, butterflies and bees.

Surprising spiders

As their name suggests, this species of spider resembles a small crab – scuttling sideways and displaying their longer front legs like crabs present their pincers. Unlike most spiders, they don't weave webs. Instead, they hunt flies, butterflies and bees on flower petals, using their forelegs to seize prey.

Clever chemicals

When a white female spider moves to a bright yellow blossom, her eyes sense that she doesn't look like her immediate surroundings. To correct this, her body produces pigments, including coloured chemical compounds called 'ommochromes'. In three days or less, she's the exact yellow of the petals around her!

If she later moves to a white flower, her body breaks down the yellow-causing pigments and she returns to white. This direction of colour change seems to be harder to do and takes a longer time – upwards of 11 days.

A female's body produces pigments that help her change colour.

A SCIENTIFIC MYSTERY

Scientists originally assumed that the female flower crab spider's special skill was needed to improve her chances of catching insects and help her avoid being eaten by predators. But there isn't much evidence to support this theory. Perhaps her camouflaging capability is linked to being female, as only female spiders have colour-coordinating powers.

Brilliantly bright birds

Eclectus parrot

The rich cobalt-blue, dazzling ruby and regal purple feathers of female eclectus parrots have baffled scientists for years. Female birds are usually coloured to camouflage themselves, but these females stand out from the crowd. They look so brightly coloured and so different from green male eclectus parrots that they were once thought to be a different species!

These females use their unusual colouring to gain attention, making sure everyone knows not to mess with their territory.

Eclectus parrot chicks start life with grey feathers.

Eye-catching colours

The answer to the puzzle of this female parrot's vivid colouring lies in her competitive lifestyle. Females don't build nests, instead raising their young in tree hollows in the rainforests of Indonesia, Papua New Guinea and Australia.

There aren't enough nesting hollows for every bird, so when a female eclectus parrot finds a hollow, it's vital she signals to nearby birds: 'This is mine, stay away!' Sitting in her tree, her eye-catching technicolour plumage – red, blue and purple against the green of the rainforest canopy – helps her to communicate this message as loudly as possible.

Stay away!

Once she's visually claimed her hollow, a female eclectus parrot's job is to guard her family and their home. For up to 11 months, she relies on different males to bring food to her – males are green in order to hide from predators as they search for fruit in the rainforest canopy.

A mother eclectus parrot will battle to the death to protect her chicks and her home! If another female intrudes and tries to move in, the two will fight fiercely, inflicting terrible beak injuries in brawls that sometimes end in death. Female eclectus parrots are bright, bold and brave!

Teenage tricksters

Orchid mantis

If you want the perfect example of how looks can deceive, check out the female orchid mantis. A teenage female resembles a delicate flower, with petal-shaped legs decked out in gorgeous shades of pink, purple, white and yellow. But don't let her appearance fool you. This youngster is a ruthless meat-eater with more than one weapon in her armoury!

Don't be fooled by this female's appearance – they are much more dangerous than they look!

Female orchid mantises attack butterflies, bees and sometimes even male mantises.

Hiding in plain sight

By looking like a nectar-rich blossom, a female orchid mantis fools inquisitive insects into thinking she's harmless. This trick is an example of 'aggressive mimicry' – the female orchid mantis uses her looks to lure her prey. When butterflies and bees come close, she strikes with lightning speed. Grasping her victim with muscular, serrated forelegs, her super-sharp mandibles (jaws) slice through her kill. While female orchid mantises are unafraid to stand out, males are smaller and less vibrant to avoid being eaten by other animals (or sometimes by female mantises)!

A deadly surprise

A female boasts a second, more subtle, weapon. She sends out airborne chemicals from her mandibles, attracting local bees in her native rainforests of Southeast Asia. These are the same chemicals which bees produce to communicate with each other, telling hive mates: 'Come here'. The mantis' cunning combination of colour and chemicals means some bees prefer to visit her over a real flower! But they get a nasty surprise when she quickly overpowers and devours them.

A newborn female is red and black.

DISGUISED FROM BIRTH

Female orchid mantises are mistresses of disguise throughout their lives. When they first hatch, they're bright red and black, resembling the venomous and foul-tasting assassin bug. 'Keep back', they signal! In adulthood, females gain considerable bulk and showcase paler hues of pink, white and yellow. Strong, deadly and colourful!

Supportive sisterhoods

Bonobo

Knowing your friends will *always* have your back is key to a female bonobo's sociable life in the African rainforest. Strong friendships between female bonobos, both young and old, are also why females lead, despite being slightly smaller than males.

Bonding behaviours

Bonobos live in groups of 100 or more female and male apes, communicating using a mixture of sounds, facial expressions and gestures. Generally more outgoing than males, females support each other by clustering together, sharing food and grooming each other by picking bugs out of their friends' fur with their fingers or mouth.

Female bonobos also frequently rub their pelvises together – a unique way of strengthening their special bond!

Keeping control

Bonobos forage for ripe fruits and plants every day and it's older, high-ranking females who usually lead the way – other bonobos watch for their movement before following themselves! Once food is found, the elevated status the females hold means they eat first; males must wait.

If a male bonobo acts aggressively while waiting for a meal, an older female will quickly gather a bonobo girl gang to sort out the squabble. The group of females use physical force, like biting, to communicate that they are in control. Males always back down after being faced with a collective display of female power!

Bonobo girl gangs aren't afraid to get physical to keep control of the group.

Taking the top spots

At night-time, bonobos bend and weave branches and leaves together to make a comfy platform bed (they use larger leaves as a blanket or hat if needed). Female bonobos remind males of their superior status by selecting safe spots high in the rainforest canopy, away from predators like leopards. Males must make their bed in a lower location, closer to potential danger.

Female bonobos like to groom each other's fur.

Hard-working honeybees

Giant honeybee

It's up to all-female worker giant honeybees to defend their mega honeycomb when it is threatened by predators or honey thieves. They, along with their queen bee, are the only members of their large family with stingers! Calling out to their sister bees, workers use vibrational and chemical communication to rapidly prepare for an attack.

Shimmering signals

Masses of female workers sit in layers in a 'bee curtain' on their honeycomb's surface. When danger is spotted, they send a powerful 'go away' message to attackers, in a spectacular vibrational event known as 'shimmering'. First, one female lifts the back of her body, and then another follows her signal, and another. Hundreds quickly join in to form a mesmerising, vibrating wave passing over the top of the honeycomb.

All-female worker bees must be communication hotshots to scare off attackers!

OUT IN THE OPEN

Instead of sheltering inside hollow trees or a hive, these South Asian bees live in the open. Their enormous honeycombs can be up to 1.5 metres wide and hang from branches, cliffs or even buildings.

Sudden swarming

If a shimmering display isn't enough to scare away an enemy, worker bees release an alarm chemical from their stinger. This chemical signals sister bees to strike! Within seconds, thousands of females fly off in a swarm to surround and sting the invader.

If they're fighting a tough-skinned hornet, the bees 'heat-ball' instead, vibrating their flight muscles to create enough combined heat to kill the hornet!

Females work together to kill a hornet.

Waggling around

Female giant honeybees also use body movements to tell fellow females about a great flower patch. This special waggle dance involves a bee shaking her tummy from side-to-side and dancing in a figure of eight shape. Her gestures reveal how far away the plants are and in what direction. The more energetic and long-lasting her dance, the better the pollen and the nectar!

Worker bees tell each other where the best flowers are.

Talking treasures of the ocean

Bottlenose dolphin

Bottlenose dolphin mums are highly sociable, fiercely intelligent communication specialists. They have to be: the special bond between females and their calves is the cornerstone of female-led dolphin pods. Mums are responsible for all calf-care, including sharing key – and remarkable – survival skills.

JUST LIKE US
Bottlenose dolphins use signature whistles to stay in contact in the same way humans use names. They are, alongside humans, elephants and marmosets, one of the only species known to communicate this way.

Underwater voices

Female bottlenose dolphins, like humans, usually give birth to one baby at a time and, like humans, these mothers also sing to their babies before and after birth. But the sounds that bottlenose dolphin mums make are very particular. A dolphin mum must ensure her baby knows mum's signature whistle – the distinctive sound identifying her – in order to keep her calf safe.

Calling to calves

After her calf is born, a female bottlenose dolphin has another clever communication trick. She tweaks her signature tune when chatting to her baby, using a higher pitch and a wider pitch range; it's akin to 'motherese' – babytalk – the singsong way human parents speak with babies. Only female dolphins use 'motherese' and it's thought to grab her calf's attention, help it learn vocal signals and cement the bond between mum and calf.

Bottlenose dolphins are fiercely intelligent communication specialists.

Dolphins can also snap their jaws together to create sound.

CLICKS AND WHISTLES

Dolphins make noise underwater using phonic (or sonic) 'lips' which sit below their blowhole. Sounds are produced when both pairs of sonic lips vibrate.

Mimicking mum

Living in the ocean, communication with sound is vital. If a calf is lost it will mimic its mum's signature whistle to find her, or mums will retrieve wandering calves by using a mixture of their maternal signature whistle and additional clicks and whistles. When calves hear this distinctive call, they know to swim back to the safety of their mum.

Songbirds with a surprising weapon

Superb lyrebird

Deep in the Australian rainforest, one female songbird has an astonishing – and loud – range of calls. Not only are female superb lyrebirds capable of sounding like multiple other bird species, they also copy other sounds, like tree branches creaking and even chainsaws buzzing!

A change of tune

For a long time, female bird song was thought to be meaningless and not worth learning about. However, it's now known that female superb lyrebirds, and many other female birds, are gifted vocalists.

For a long time, no one knew how powerful female bird song was.

Male lyrebirds are good imitators too, but they make noise mostly to show off to partners. A female uses sound as a weapon! Her song is piercing because protecting her family and defending her territory is a female's job alone – and it's *hard* work.

VERSATILE VOCALS

As a bird breathes out, air passes through its voice box and sound is created. Lyrebirds have a more complex voice box and can control airflow from each lung. Their fantastic voice box allows them to create an extraordinary range of sounds.

Superb lyrebird chick

Survival song

A female lays one precious egg at a time, looking after her chick for several months after it hatches. During this time, it is mum's stunning vocal skills which shield the two of them.

If her nest is threatened, a mother lyrebird copies the calls of local birds of prey to create the illusion that danger is nearby. She also mimics 'mob calls' – noises birds make to summon help for an attack. When foraging for food, she blasts out an alarm song – whistling: 'Stay away!' If her calls are ignored, she charges, using her strong, clawed feet to wound. The message is clear: don't mess with this musical mum!

Multi-talented music makers

◀◀◀◀◀◀◀◀ *African clawed frog* ▶▶▶▶▶▶▶▶

Finding a partner at the right time in a crowded, murky pond isn't easy. Luckily, female African clawed frogs can use rare vocal talents to attract their perfect match. When this aquatic female wants to get together with a male, she lets those nearby know by blasting out an underwater song!

MUSCLES AND CARTILAGE

The songs of African clawed frogs can only be heard faintly in the air but are very clear underwater. These frogs don't have vocal cords but instead sing by vibrating the discs of their larynx (or voice box). These discs are made of cartilage – tissue which is also found in the human nose! A female's larynx has more slow-twitch muscles that can support her rapping and ticking, and females can also make lower frequency sounds than males.

A female calls out to a male underwater.

Romantic beats

Her aquatic music is intense and powerful – imagine short, swift beats, a bit like speedy hammer-tapping or the sound of a wooden percussion instrument. Her loud rhythm is hard to miss, and a potential partner responds immediately by calling out to her. As they swim towards each other, they create a romantic duet.

Close-up of African clawed frog eggs.

This frog makes sure her message is heard loud and clear, even if she's singing underwater!

Ticked off

Female African clawed frogs have another tune in their repertoire called 'ticking', which consists of slower, thud-like sounds. It is the opposite of a romantic song and instead advises a keen male that a female is completely uninterested in him! When male frogs hear her 'tick', they get her message loud and clear and leave her alone.

African clawed frog tadpoles

A quick match

To date, the female African clawed frog is one of only a few female frogs known to sing to locate a mate. She is skilled at doing this because timing is vital for her success in starting a family. She only has a short window of time to find a partner before the thousands of eggs she is carrying will go to waste.

Earth's expert explorers

Green turtle

Every five years or so, adult female green turtles embark on an epic oceanic adventure. Leaving their feeding grounds along the coasts of Brazil, Mexico and the United States of America, they set out across the open ocean to distant beaches in places such as Ascension Island and the Seychelles.

A journey which involves spending six weeks alone at sea and swimming more than 3,200 kilometres, it is one of the most awe-inspiring feats of navigation in the entire animal queendom.

An adult female digs a nest.

The perfect place

Female green turtles complete this extraordinary quest because they're looking for the beach they were born on years earlier! Once there, they'll dig a 1-metre-deep nest with their hind flippers and carefully lay around 100 eggs. It's not an easy task but females are large and strong. They need to be bigger and stronger than their male partners: after several weeks of egg laying, females must make the tough return swim back across the ocean.

Female green turtles go on epic adventures, using Earth's magnetic field as their guide.

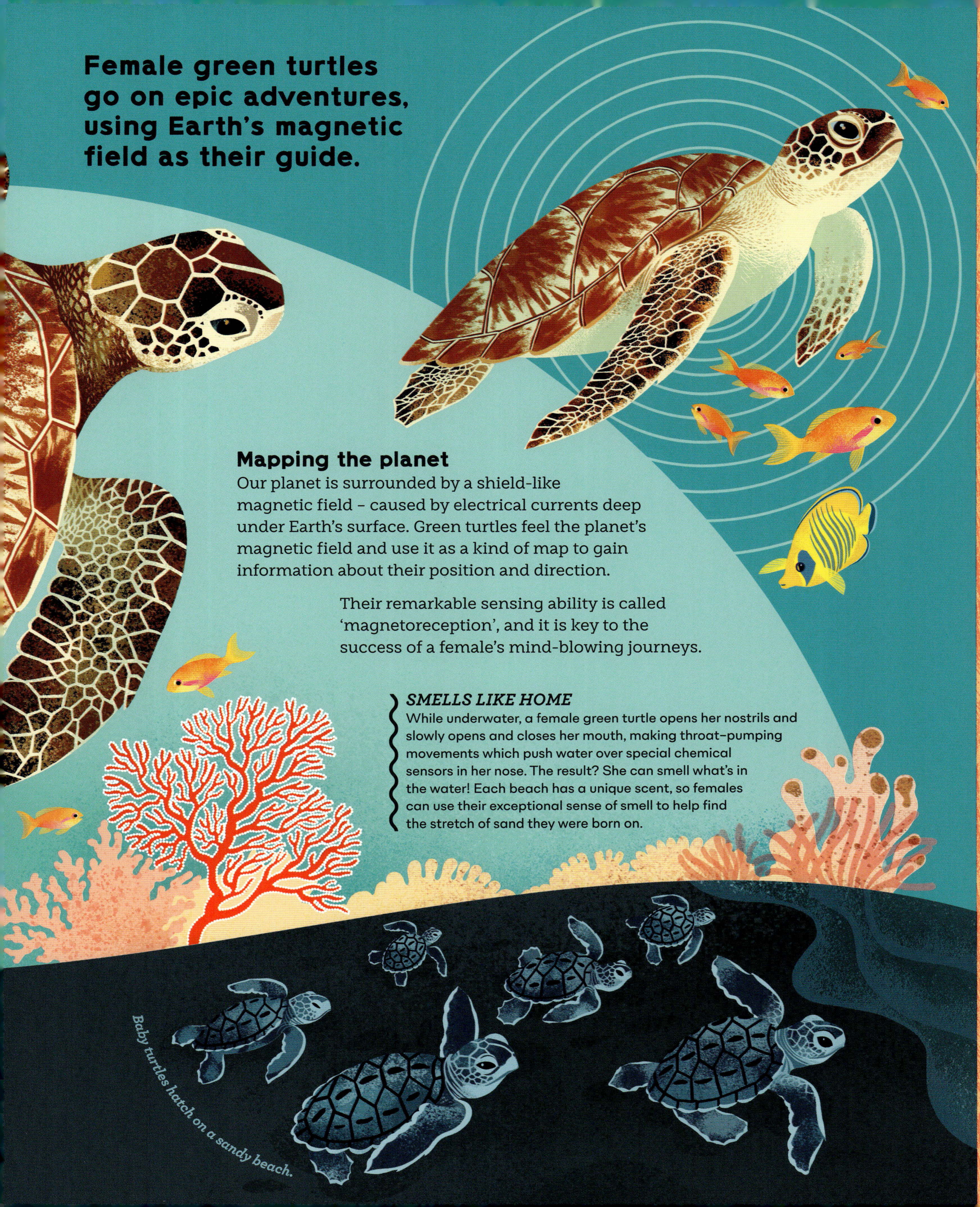

Mapping the planet

Our planet is surrounded by a shield-like magnetic field – caused by electrical currents deep under Earth's surface. Green turtles feel the planet's magnetic field and use it as a kind of map to gain information about their position and direction.

Their remarkable sensing ability is called 'magnetoreception', and it is key to the success of a female's mind-blowing journeys.

SMELLS LIKE HOME

While underwater, a female green turtle opens her nostrils and slowly opens and closes her mouth, making throat-pumping movements which push water over special chemical sensors in her nose. The result? She can smell what's in the water! Each beach has a unique scent, so females can use their exceptional sense of smell to help find the stretch of sand they were born on.

Baby turtles hatch on a sandy beach.

FULL OF FEMALES

Ant societies are primarily female. An ant queen rules the colony and can have up to 150 million daughters in her lifetime! All worker ants are female and all sisters, while males are only born at certain times of the year.

Ant colonies contain millions of ants, all ruled by a queen.

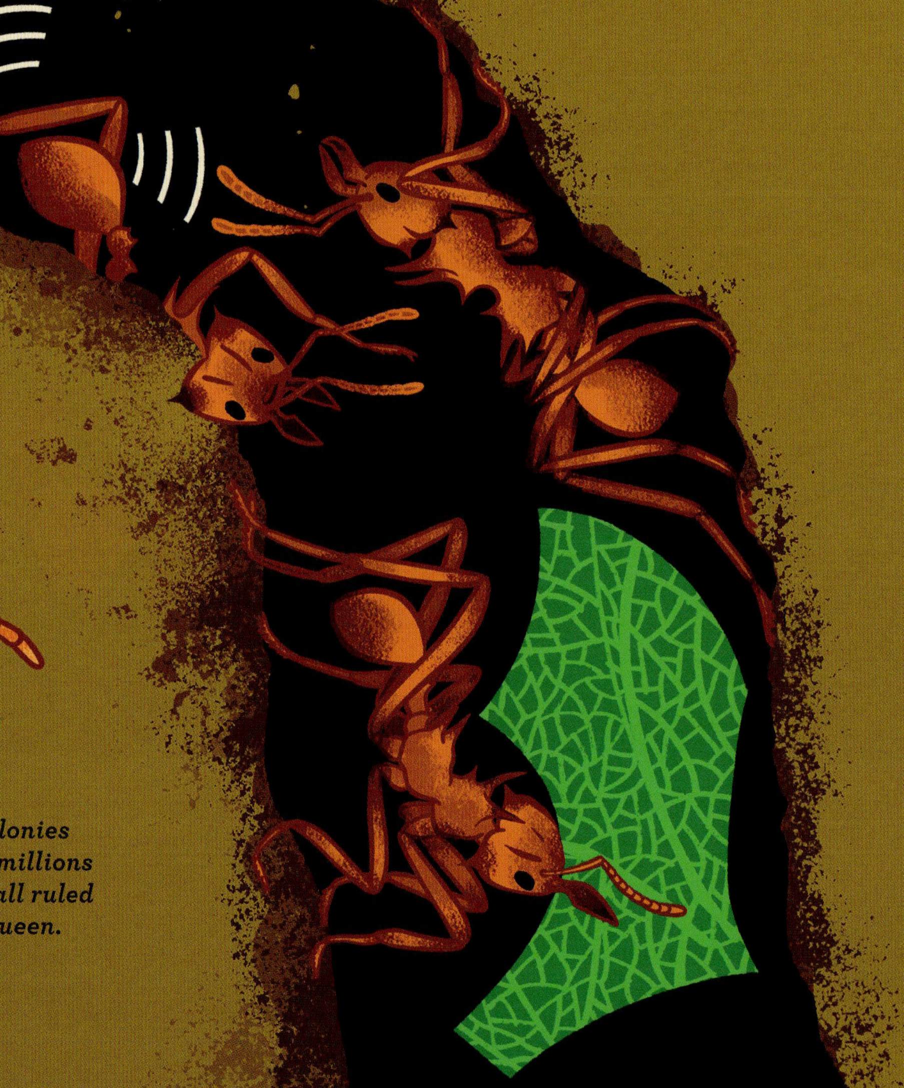

Shouting out

Workers rely on vibrational chat to recruit their sisters' help in other situations. Ants carrying leaves are at risk of flies infecting them with harmful parasites, so they stridulate, or 'shout out', for assistance. Smaller worker sisters (called 'minims') then hitch a ride on the leaf, cleaning it and guarding foragers from fly attack.

Workers also use their vibratory sense to rapidly call for help if they're in a fight, or to signal for rescue if they're buried underground. Strong vibrations and sisters save the day!

Signal-sensing sisters

Leafcutter ant

Worker leafcutter ants are known as the weight-lifting wonders of the rainforest, capable of carrying leaves much heavier than themselves. But these all-female workers would not be able to gather this food so easily without their exceptional vibratory sense, which they use to 'hear', understand and locate each other's key vibrational signals!

A female leafcutter ant sends vibrational signals to other workers.

Surprisingly strong

Worker leafcutter ants forage for leaves, cutting them into pieces with their strong jaws. They then carry segments many times their size and weight back to their underground nest (the ants can't digest the leaves but instead use them to grow a fungus they can eat). When an ant locates a fresh leaf, it's time to use her special sense!

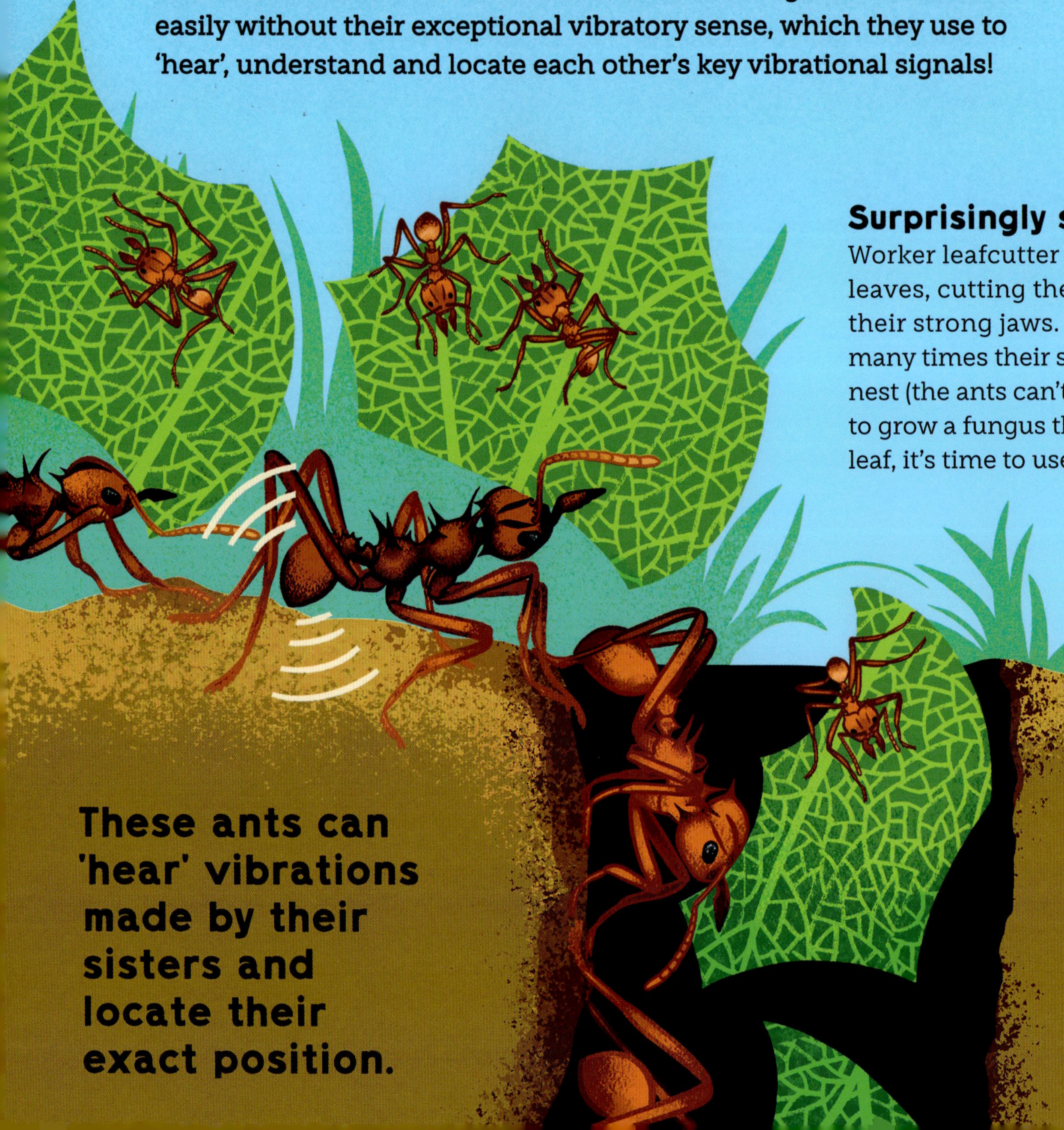

These ants can 'hear' vibrations made by their sisters and locate their exact position.

Good vibrations

She creates a vibrating message by rubbing together her 'scraper' and 'file' – part of a smart bit of kit on her lower belly called her 'stridulatory organ'. The pulsating signals travel through her body and into the leaf she's cutting. Workers up to 30 centimetres away pick up these vibrations via specialised sensors in each of their 6 legs. Astonishingly, worker ants can identify the location of the message sender by recognising whether their left or right set of legs receives the vibrations first!

Sensitive sound-seekers

Common vampire bat

All bats have great hearing, but common vampire bats – famous for only feeding on blood – can hear low frequency noise that others can't. As these low frequency sounds travel over longer distances, this species can hear stirrings from further away than other bats. Female vampire bats use this super-sense to find bat pups and female friends, and to search out sleeping victims to feed on!

Keeping in contact

Vampire bats live in mainly female colonies of up to 300 or more bats. When a female bat returns to her dark home after a night-time's hunting, she uses her extra-sensitive low frequency hearing to recognise her pup's 'contact call' out of hundreds of other bats. She then feeds her hungry youngster by regurgitating blood into its mouth!

EXTRA-SHARP EARS

Most bats use echolocation to find their way and avoid bumping into objects. Echolocation involves creating high frequency sound pulses and listening for the echo from those sounds. Vampire bats have even more exceptional *low* frequency hearing than other bats, using these sounds for hunting and communication.

Friends in need

Female vampire bats are very friendly, forming relationships with other females that can last for years. They use their special hearing to pick out their pals' low frequency contact calls and will fly to them. They'll even feed starving females. It's thought they sense a friend's hunger from the noise she makes and her begging behaviour – the ravenous bat licks her full friend's lips!

These females can recognise the calls of friends and pups out of hundreds of other bat sounds!

Blood-sucking senses

Vampire bats only feed on sleeping prey and it's their low frequency hearing which enables them to sense snoozing sounds from far away. Once located, vampire bats use a blood-sucking sense called 'thermoception'. Heat-sensing 'pit organs' on their nose detect differences in their prey's body temperature – a hot spot shows blood flow near the skin's surface and indicates the best place to bite.

Vampire bats can sense the best place to bite their prey.

Poisonous plant-finders

Queen Alexandra's birdwing

Deep in the forests of Papua New Guinea, the world's biggest butterfly can be found drumming her six feet on leaves and vines. She is the Queen Alexandra's birdwing, and she can use extraordinary senses in her feet and legs to find a particular plant!

LARGEST BUTTERFLY ON EARTH

Butterfly chrysalis

Tasting with your feet

Butterflies taste the world through chemical receptors, or sense cells, on their feet, legs and antennae. Humans have similar tasting receptors on our tongue and in our nose. Female butterflies are super-sensitive at tasting plants because they have extra 'taste hairs' – spines on the tips of their forelegs. When a female pounds her feet on a plant and stomps out its sap, she senses more taste information.

SIZE COMPARISON

RECORD BREAKER

If no one wants to eat you, then you have the chance to become the largest butterfly on Earth! Bigger and stronger than a male, a female Queen Alexandra's birdwing has a colossal wingspan measuring up to 30 centimetres. If one landed on you, she would cover your chest!

By using her senses to find one special plant, this butterfly helps her children become poisonous!

Queen Alexandra's birdwing with wings fully open.

Searching for perfection

Female butterflies have superpowered taste senses because they must find the perfect plants to lay their eggs and have future caterpillar children feed on. Queen Alexandra's birdwing females are looking for just one specific forest plant. The leafy climbing vine in question, called *Aristolochia schlecteri*, is very poisonous!

Queen Alexandra's birdwing caterpillar

TOXIC CHILDREN

Giving your babies a dangerous meal seems strange. However, this female's senses help her make a smart choice. When her caterpillars munch on the vine, they don't become sick like other animals do. Instead, they take the toxins into their bodies and they, and the butterflies they turn into, become poisonous. The result? Would-be predators avoid eating them.

Leaders with life-saving memories

African bush elephant

Matriarchs are the great leaders of elephant societies: females with the skill and experience to save the herd in times of crisis. The older these leaders are, the better they are at the job. Females can live into their seventies!

Head of the herd

The oldest and largest female bush elephant is usually matriarch to family groups of 50 or more, made up of the leader's adult female relatives and everyone's calves. While these groups often mix with other families to form clans, males leave the herd at puberty and lead largely isolated lives on the African plains.

Matriarchs take charge in protecting calves from danger.

Experienced elders

Elephants travel long distances daily searching for grasses, water holes and shade. The matriarch typically walks at the front of the herd, indicating a direction change by facing the way she wants to go, lifting one foot and making a low 'let's go' rumble sound. Herds pay attention – at times of drought, it's older matriarchs who recall the location of remote water holes which may not have been visited for many years.

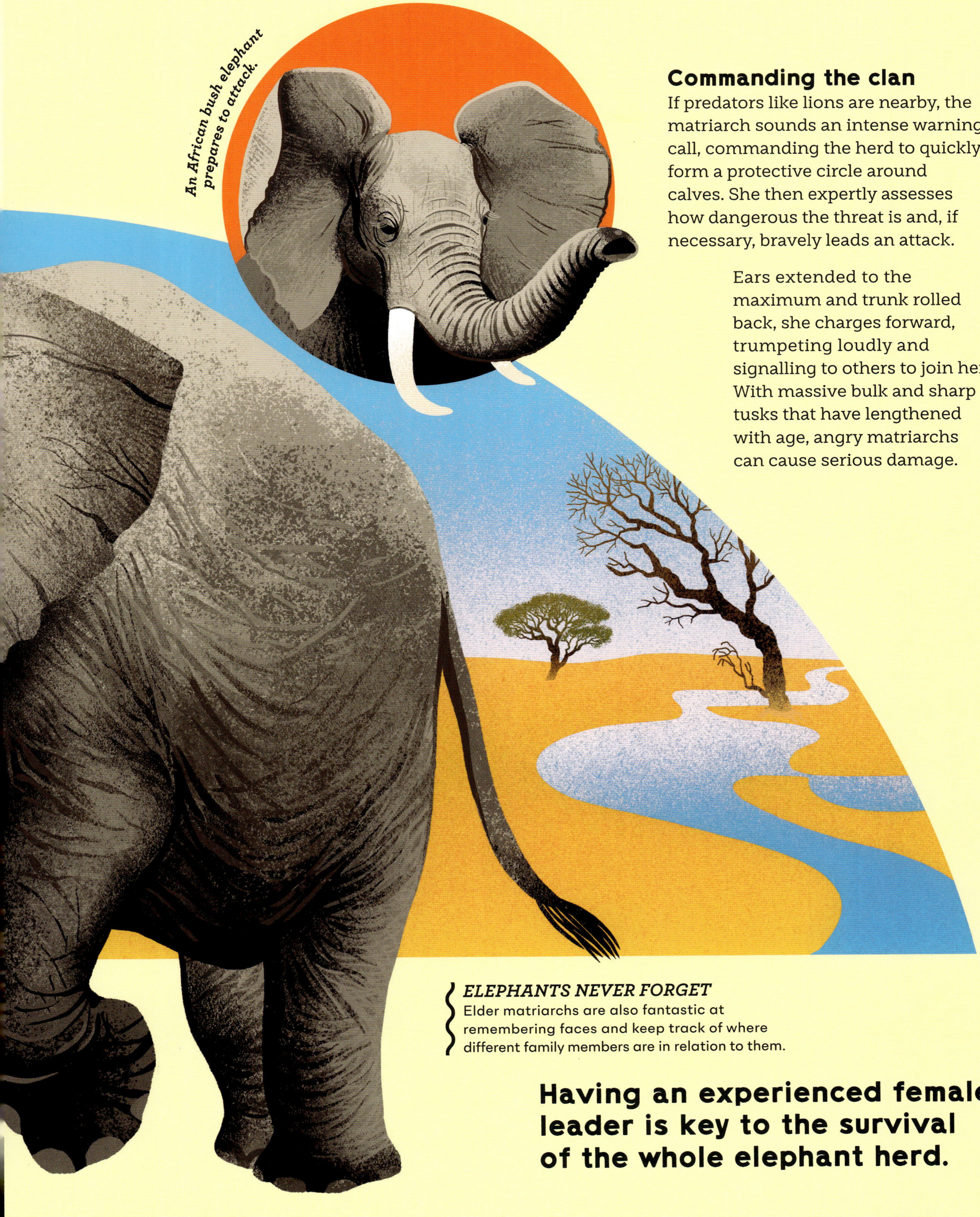

Commanding the clan

If predators like lions are nearby, the matriarch sounds an intense warning call, commanding the herd to quickly form a protective circle around calves. She then expertly assesses how dangerous the threat is and, if necessary, bravely leads an attack.

Ears extended to the maximum and trunk rolled back, she charges forward, trumpeting loudly and signalling to others to join her. With massive bulk and sharp tusks that have lengthened with age, angry matriarchs can cause serious damage.

ELEPHANTS NEVER FORGET

Elder matriarchs are also fantastic at remembering faces and keep track of where different family members are in relation to them.

Having an experienced female leader is key to the survival of the whole elephant herd.

Magnificent mentors

Orca

Whether it's remembering where to find food or knowing the best hunting strategies, the wisdom and leadership of an older female orca is key to the success of her whale pod. Female orcas live remarkably long lives, up to 90 years or more, while males live for around 50 years!

Leading the way

Orca pods can have different diets, but knowing where to locate fish is crucial for salmon-eating orcas. Pods rely on a matriarch's long memory to guide them to the right spots, particularly when food is scarce.

The female leader swims at the front of the pod, rising up and slapping her two-metre-wide tail flukes on the ocean surface to command the pod to change direction.

With an older female in their lives, younger orcas are far more likely to survive.

Active attacks

Orca hunts for gray whale calves can be complicated, taking up to five hours of effort! The pod must work together to catch their prey, but it's active adult females who start the attack, biting the calf and swimming on top of its blowhole to smother it before it can escape.

LONG-TERM LEADERS

Even after they have passed along vast knowledge, the leadership of an older female orca can make the difference between life and death for a pod. With her in their lives, her children are far more likely to survive.

Orcas snatch seals lying on beaches.

Survival skills

Snatching lazing seals or sea lions from beaches is a smart orca hunting tactic, but it's extremely dangerous – one wrong move and orcas can be stranded on the sand. It's up to female leaders to teach calves the skills needed to grab their prey, and to save them if they get in trouble! By accelerating rapidly towards the shore and then suddenly stopping and turning, adult females have figured out how to generate a wave big enough to rescue a stuck calf!

Protectors of the pride

African lioness

Forget *The Lion King* – it's lionesses who lead the pride! Lions are the friendliest of the big cats and the only ones to live in tight-knit family groups. Prides always have more female lions than males, and adult females are all related. Most prides will include up to 21 lionesses, everyone's cubs, and a handful of unrelated adult males.

Dream teams

Lionesses hunt as a team, share the prey they catch and work together to defend the pride's territory against intruders. Female pridemates don't fight with each other, but lionesses do clash with neighbouring prides over land. Each pride wants to rule land with plenty of tasty zebra to catch, so that no one goes hungry.

Perfect predators

Lionesses are designed to be hunters: female lions are faster than males, and they're also better at blending into their surroundings. A team of lionesses on the savannahs and grasslands of Sub-Saharan Africa is a fearsome sight.

Each lioness has a favourite hunting position. Some are on the 'wing' in stalking roles and will begin a charge. Other lionesses take a central spot and have the job of capturing prey as it flees. Male lions scavenge from kills and don't help as much when part of the hunt.

A CLUB FOR CUBS

Lion cubs join a group nursery, where they can be breastfed by multiple mothers. Caring for cubs collectively protects young lions from outside attacks. Teamwork is tops for the queen of cats!

Lionesses make life-or-death decisions for their pride – where to move, what to eat and how to defend their territory.

Queens who call the shots

Ring-tailed lemur

In the forests of southern Madagascar, it's female ring-tailed lemurs who call the shots. These cat-sized primates, with their distinctive black-and-white stripy tails, are fierce bullies who fight with and boss around male lemurs. Their queen is the most vicious of all!

Top of the troop

Ring-tailed lemurs live in troops of between 12 and 24 adult females, males and junior lemurs. Every troop member knows to give way to the queen – the alpha female. If the queen wants the sunniest spot to nap in, she'll take it. If she fancies the fruit that another lemur has, she'll lunge and snatch it.

She's typically one of the oldest lemurs and the most violent – she's earned her top position by coming first in fights.

Every lemur in the troop knows to get out of the queen's way.

Fierce and feisty

Female lemurs are feisty even as infants, starting most rough-and-tumble play and slamming males on their backs during playful fights. This behaviour is the start of females building a more powerful position in the troop. It's thought female lemurs are more aggressive so that they have the status to command more food during pregnancy and motherhood.

PUT IN THEIR PLACE!

Although female and male lemurs are the same size, all adult females enjoy a higher status than males. Females usually best males when challenged or cause them to back away. If an adult male annoys a female, she'll tug his tail or bite or hit his ear or head!

The cost of combat

Female lemurs benefit from fighting, but there's a downside to their combative nature.

When a lemur mum fights, her youngsters are often clinging to her. Going into battle with your baby is far from ideal, and infants are hurt falling to the ground or attacked and killed. For warring females, ruling with an iron fist can be very costly.

Orangutans learn to craft umbrellas out of leaves.

Mother orangutans spend at least a decade raising their babies, helping them to survive life in the rainforest.

TERRIFIC TEACHING

Spending so much time with mum means young orangutans also learn to craft things to help them in other parts of their lives. They can create a comfy tree bed, fashion an umbrella from a bunch of leafy branches, or even use leaves as toilet paper to wipe off poo!

Clever caregivers

Orangutans are thought to be the most intelligent primate after humans, and years spent together with mum mean far more orangutans reach adulthood than other wild apes. Smart mothers and non-stop childcare save lives!

Gentle guardians

Orangutan

The prize for hardest-working animal parent goes to the planet's largest tree-living mammal – the orangutan. Mother orangutans take on solo responsibility for all childcare, providing hands-on help for youngsters until they're at least 10 years old! Humans are the only ape who look after their children for longer.

A lot to learn

Orangutan females have one baby about every eight years and infants spend their first years clinging to their mother's fabulous red fur. Mums spend so much time with their baby because young orangutans have to learn a lot to survive. They must become experts at moving between trees high in the rainforests of Malaysia and Indonesia – sometimes it's okay to jump, other times it's better to sway trees back and forth or pull smaller branches over until a bigger, sturdier one is reached.

Watch and learn

Food in the rainforest is often scarce and can be tricky to get to. Young orangutans watch their skilled mothers make tools – and then copy their movements. Clever mums strip leaves and twigs from branches to make a perfect stick for pulling out honey and termites from tree holes, or fruit and seeds from plants. They even create leaf gloves to protect their hands from spiky fruit!

Mighty marine mammals

Blue whale

LARGEST ANIMAL ON EARTH

The female blue whale is the biggest animal on the planet, regularly reaching 30 metres in length. Imagine three double-decker buses end to end and you'll have an idea of her size! These record-breaking queens of the ocean are the most massive mums on Earth, and their size helps them take good care of their giant children.

Close-up of a blue whale eye.

RECORD BREAKER

Move over dinosaurs... The female blue whale holds the record for the most massive animal to have EVER lived! The biggest recorded female blue whale was 33 metres long – more than a third bigger than the average male – and the heaviest ever was 190 tonnes (about the weight of 30 elephants).

Colossal calves

Blue whales have one baby at a time and they are the world's biggest and heaviest: a calf can be a whopping 8 metres long and weigh 3.5 tonnes. Calves are completely dependent on their mother for the first six months of life, so having the most mighty mum on Earth is essential.

Blue whale mums use their massive size to successfully parent the world's fastest growing babies.

A mother's milk

Astonishingly, blue whale mothers eat very little or not at all when they are breastfeeding their baby. Instead, they rely on the 45 tonnes of stored blubber they build up from eating krill over their months of pregnancy. They can produce around 220 litres of milk (enough to fill a bath and more) every day for their hungry newborn! Thanks to her super-rich milk, a blue whale is mum to the world's fastest growing infant – increasing by nearly a tonne every 10 days.

Blue whale calves nudge their mother to signal that they want milk.

Protective parents

In springtime, a blue whale mum and calf swim together from winter feeding grounds to summer ones. Mum guides them on their journey and, if her curious calf gets too close to a ship, she'll place herself between the calf and the potential danger.

She also lets her tired youngster 'back-ride' by touching or swimming very close to her back, allowing them to save energy and be propelled along in mum's slipstream.

Incredibly caring insects

European earwig

There's a very special club in the insect world: the surprisingly small percentage of parents who look after their offspring. The female European earwig is a top member! Most insects leave their eggs to hatch alone. But European earwigs are astonishingly devoted – and fierce – mothers who go above and beyond to protect their young.

Earwigs enjoy eating dahlias.

Patient parents

In autumn, a female earwig builds an underground nest in soil and lays up to 70 oval, cream-coloured eggs. She guards her eggs for months until they hatch, not even stopping to eat!

Guarding is not easy. Her eggs lie in soil exposed to bacteria and fungi which can destroy them, so she uses her mouthparts to continuously clean the eggs and coat them with a protective chemical. If her nest is disturbed and her eggs are scattered, or if the burrow gets too cold for her eggs to develop, she painstakingly picks up each egg in her mouth and moves everyone to a better, warmer home.

A female earwig attacks a spider.

Fierce fighters

An earwig mum furiously defends her eggs from attack by spiders or other earwigs. She's larger and more aggressive than male earwigs, and has impressive weaponry. Sticking out from her bendy abdomen is a pair of scissor-like pincers, which she raises above her head or to the side to scare attackers away.

If this doesn't work, she rapidly strikes out with her pincers, cutting small spiders in half and spraying them with a disgusting-smelling chemical!

Snack time!

After months of keeping her eggs safe, they're ready to hatch into earwig nymphs. An earwig mum's final task is providing food but, luckily, nymphs are not fussy eaters. They enjoy munching on the plant pieces and small aphids mum brings, but also happily swallow food regurgitated from her mouth.

It's very rare for insects to look after their young, but mother earwigs are determined to keep their children safe.

SUPPORTIVE TO THE END

This intrepid insect mum can help her children survive in one other strange way. If she dies unexpectedly, her nymphs will eat her body!

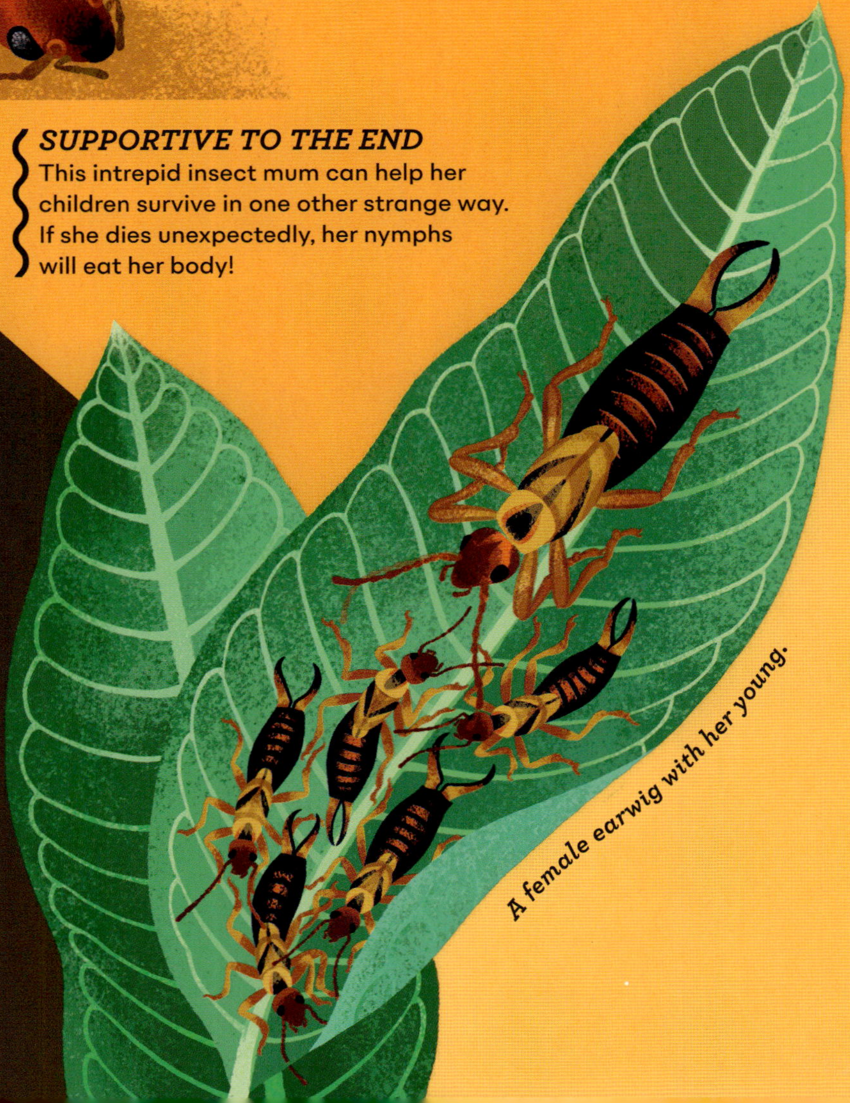

A female earwig with her young.

Lightning-fast families

Cheetah

FASTEST LAND ANIMAL ON EARTH

Female cheetahs have more cubs than most other big cats – sometimes raising six by themselves at one time! Being solely responsible for feeding your large family is tough, but female cheetahs have a hugely helpful record-breaking skill – they're the fastest land animal on the planet!

The need for speed

All cheetahs are exceptionally quick, but it's the slightly lighter and smaller females who run the fastest. They are built for speed, with large nostrils allowing them to take in more oxygen, slender bodies, deep chests, long legs and exceptionally flexible spines.

A mother cheetah needs to be the winner in every high-speed game of chase against a quick-moving antelope or gazelle – if she fails, her cubs will go hungry!

RECORD BREAKER

A 'polka-dotted missile'. That's a description of Sarah, the South African cheetah who set the record for the fastest recorded land animal at Cincinnati Zoo, in the United States of America, in 2012. Sarah ran 100 metres in just 5.95 seconds and accelerated from zero to 97 kilometres per hour in 3.5 seconds. It's thought wild cheetahs run even faster!

Fast feet

Thanks to their semi-retractable claws and hardened and grooved foot pads, cheetahs have fantastic traction on the ground (it's like they're wearing top-grade trainers). They showcase stunning reaction times, able to turn rapidly and make sudden stops.

These mothers have to reach breakneck speeds to make the kills needed to feed their cubs.

Going solo

Adult female cheetahs are very independent, living alone or with their cubs, while adult males stay apart in small groups. Cubs are completely dependent on mum for around two years, relying on her to protect them, feed them and teach them how to hunt food of their own.

Cubs practise hunting with wounded prey.

Hunting lessons

When her cubs are about 5 months old, mum begins to bring them animals that she's wounded rather than killed.

From an early age, it's female cubs, not males, who more often take the initiative in hunting. Presenting the wounded prey, mum allows her cubs to practise knocking down and killing their food without putting them in danger. With her help, the cubs will grow up knowing how to speedily hunt their own food, allowing them to survive long after mum is gone.

Frogs with babies on their backs

Andean marsupial tree frog

In the humid mountain forests of Ecuador, a female tree frog has a clever way of protecting her growing family. Most frogs lay their eggs in water and leave, but it's a risky strategy because lots of frogspawn is eaten by nearby predators. The Andean marsupial tree frog tries a different tactic, keeping hold of her eggs while they're developing into tadpoles. Only the female of the species can do this, because she has a nifty bit of physical kit – a froggy backpack!

Developing eggs bulge against a female's stretched pouch.

A female with an empty pouch.

Unusual baggage

This is no ordinary backpack. A pouch of special skin stretches down the female's back to a triangular opening at the base of her spine. As a mother frog lays her eggs, the father catches them with his feet and places them into her waiting pouch – which then stays tightly closed. Incredibly, it can hold up to 200 eggs and expands by up to 3 centimetres as the babies grow!

Stretched for space

Andean marsupial tree frogs shelter their young for up to four months. That's a long time for a small frog to carry hundreds of babies! Shortly before birth, the squirming tadpoles push against the pouch, stretching it until it almost looks clear.

Close-up of growing babies inside eggs.

A quick exit

When a mother is ready to 'give birth', she moves to safe water and prepares for some frog gymnastics. Lifting up her lower body, she uses her extra-long fourth toe to open her pouch and release her tadpoles into the water.

If any remain, she will put her whole foot into the pouch, reaching as far back as she can to help them out. Thanks to mum's efforts, her tadpoles get a valuable leg-up in life!

Tadpoles are released into water from their mother's pouch.

A mother carries hundreds of growing tadpoles for months, stretching her pouch until it is almost see-through.

Multi-tasking mothers

Tammar wallaby

She may be small, but Australia's female tammar wallaby is a magnificent, multi-tasking powerhouse when it comes to parenting. Wallabies have some of the quickest pregnancies in the queendom, can get pregnant immediately after giving birth and can then pause their pregnancy for months at a time!

Smaller than a sweet

A mama wallaby makes a baby at warp speed, giving birth to a joey (a baby wallaby) tinier than a jellybean after only 26 days of pregnancy. Like other young marsupial mammals – including kangaroos and koalas – wallabies will spend their first eight to nine months of life in their mother's 'marsupium', or pouch.

Baby wallaby at birth.

A perfect pocket

A female's pouch is much more than a pocket to rest in – it's a state-of-the-art nursery supplying everything a joey needs. The pouch's skin provides extra oxygen to the joey in its first few days of life, and produces compounds protecting the joey from disease-causing bacteria.

Newborn and young joeys feed from their mother's pouch.

Changing with her children

A female wallaby can feed a newborn and older joey simultaneously! As a joey feeds and grows, one of her four nipples grows with it. The nipple eventually extends out of her pouch, becoming a slim straw for a hopping joey to drink from on the ground. When this older joey doesn't feed as much, that's the signal for a baby waiting in mum's womb to begin to grow again and take its place in her pouch.

Thanks to her incredible biology, this marsupial mum can have an older joey occasionally snacking on her milk, a newborn tucked up in her pouch and a third baby on pause in her womb, all at the same time!

MIRACULOUS MILK

This awe-inspiring mum produces two *completely different* types of breast milk at the same time. One milky drink is rich in nutrients for newborn joeys. The second is altered to meet the growing needs of older joeys and contains more fats for her already or soon-to-be hopping offspring.

These wallabies' bodies allow them to raise multiple joeys at once, while growing a new baby in record time.

Self-sufficient sawfish

Smalltooth sawfish

What would you do if your species was facing possible extinction and you couldn't find a male partner to have babies with? Female smalltooth sawfish are facing this problem, but they have a seemingly miraculous solution – a superpower which males of the species don't possess. They give birth to babies without any male input!

A surprising discovery

Smalltooth sawfish are famous for their chainsaw-like snout, but unfortunately it gets easily entangled in fishing nets. Sadly, this means that they are now one of the most endangered marine fish on the planet. In 2015, scientists were very surprised to discover that, although female sawfish were still making babies with males, a small number had become super solo mums via a process called 'parthenogenesis'.

Sawfish females can have children with a male *or* completely by themselves!

Sawfish have pale undersides.

Unusual animals

This was the first time that this awesome female ability was seen in vertebrates (animals with a backbone) in the wild! Parthenogenesis is rare, estimated to occur in less than one per cent of all animal species, and never in mammals. The elite group of female animals capable of the process, to date, includes only a few species of sharks, lizards, fish, insects, snakes, scorpions, frogs and birds.

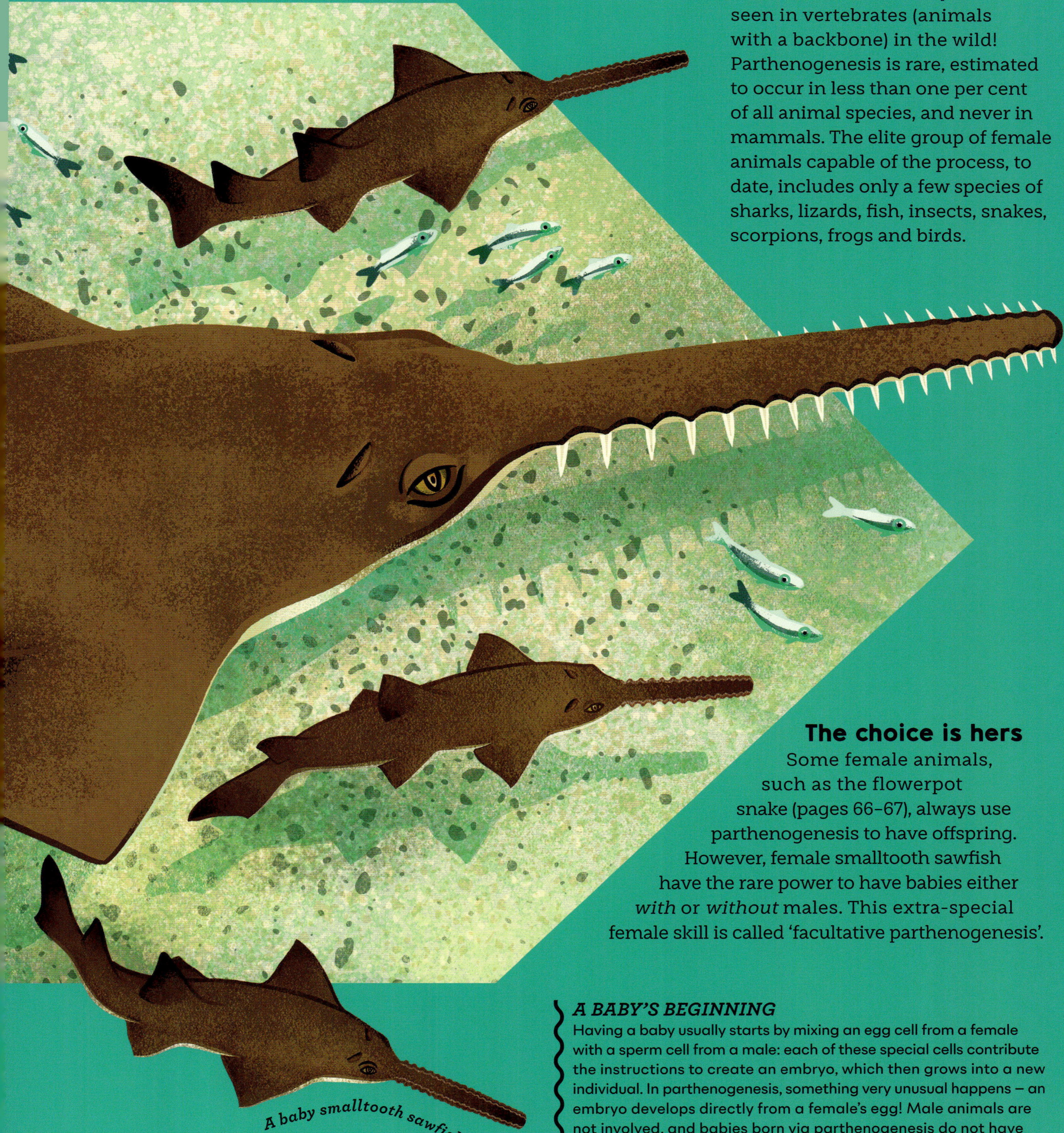

A baby smalltooth sawfish.

The choice is hers

Some female animals, such as the flowerpot snake (pages 66–67), always use parthenogenesis to have offspring. However, female smalltooth sawfish have the rare power to have babies either *with* or *without* males. This extra-special female skill is called 'facultative parthenogenesis'.

A BABY'S BEGINNING

Having a baby usually starts by mixing an egg cell from a female with a sperm cell from a male: each of these special cells contribute the instructions to create an embryo, which then grows into a new individual. In parthenogenesis, something very unusual happens – an embryo develops directly from a female's egg! Male animals are not involved, and babies born via parthenogenesis do not have dads, only superstar mums.

All-female offspring

Flowerpot snake

At 10 to 13 centimetres long, the female flowerpot snake is one of the smallest snakes on the planet. She's also the most widespread land snake in the world! This tiny, almost-blind reptile is found on almost every continent because of her incredible way of making snakelets – and her quirky habit of hiding in the soil of flowerpots.

Independent women

Flowerpot snakes often end up being accidentally transported around the globe, after sneaking into the soil of potted plants due to be shipped overseas. But when one arrives in a new country, she doesn't need to worry about finding another flowerpot snake to start a family with. That's because she possesses the unique female power of parthenogenesis: the ability to have babies *without* a male.

Only a few animals can become a mother via parthenogenesis, but the flowerpot snake is a member of an even more astounding female-only club. This group is for animal species where females are the only sex to exist! The babies that female flowerpot snakes have using parthenogenesis are always daughters, and these daughters only ever give birth to daughters. They're a spectacular, superpowered sisterhood!

Flowerpot snakes are so tiny, some people mistake them for worms.

These snakes only give birth to daughters – no males of the species have ever been found!

SPECIAL SPECIES

All-female families are very rare: there aren't any all-female mammals or all-female birds. But there are all-female frogs, salamanders, lizards, ladybirds, grasshoppers and stick insects, as well as all-female fish (the Amazon molly was the first all-female species to be found). All-female reproduction is the fastest way to forge a girls-only dynasty, either in your homeland or, like the flowerpot snake, all around the world.

Deep-sea survival stars

Northern giant seadevil

BIGGEST SIZE DIFFERENCE

Over a kilometre and a half deep in the ocean, the lack of light makes it difficult to find food or a partner. Incredibly, the female Northern giant seadevil has specifically adapted to her unusual surroundings. Thanks to her extraordinary features and massive size, she thrives in the blackness!

Designed for darkness

This anglerfish doesn't need to rely on sight in the gloomy ocean – her monstrously large head and huge jaw with rows of dagger-like teeth mean she's not going to miss any nearby fish lured by her light. Plus, her mouth, throat and stomach have adapted to stretch so that she can swallow sea creatures whole!

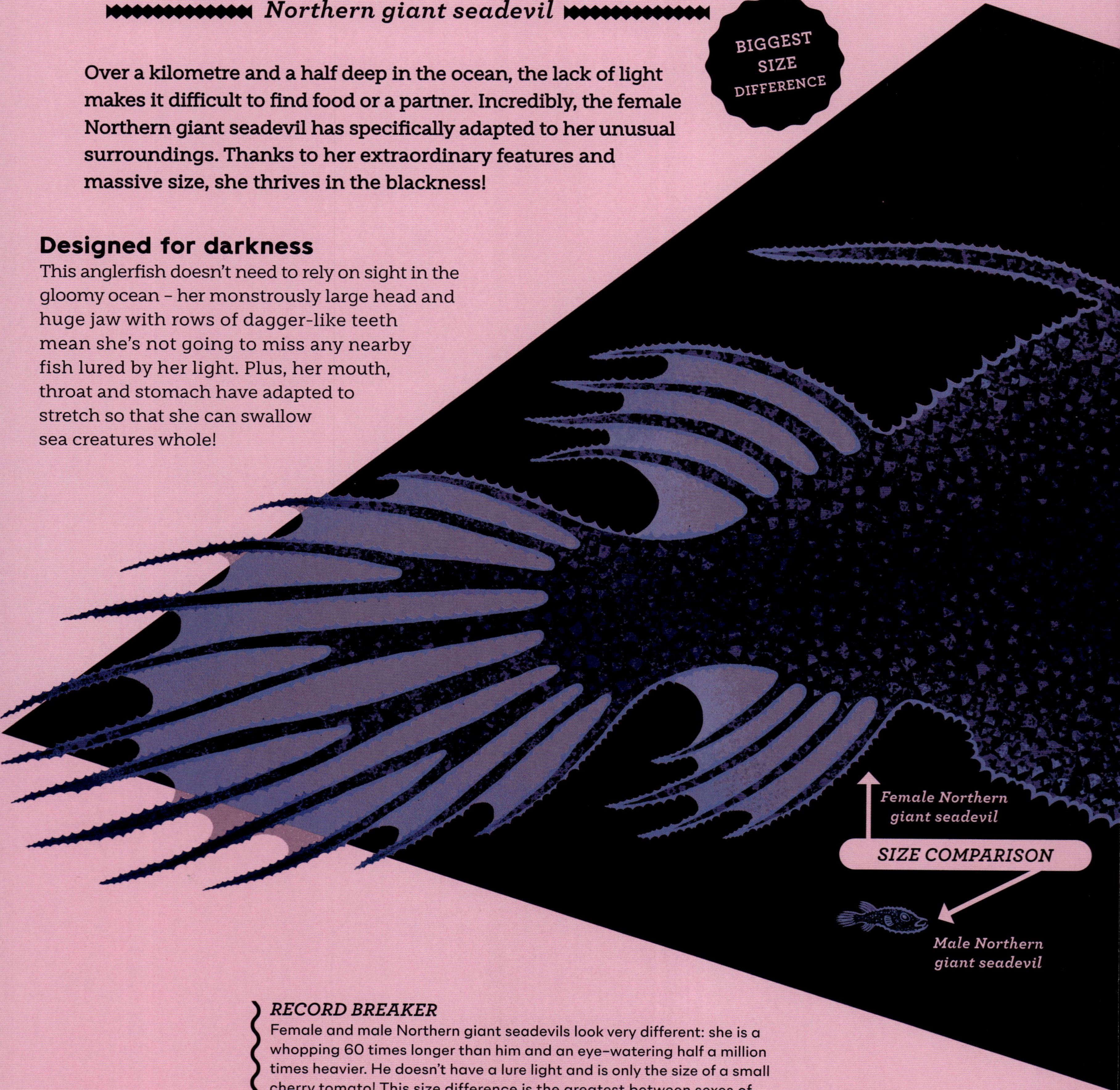

RECORD BREAKER

Female and male Northern giant seadevils look very different: she is a whopping 60 times longer than him and an eye-watering half a million times heavier. He doesn't have a lure light and is only the size of a small cherry tomato! This size difference is the greatest between sexes of the same species with a backbone. The female is so big compared to the male that we can't show their sizes exactly to scale here.

A female's body is perfectly adapted to hunting in the deep ocean, while males must rely on females for survival.

Fooling her prey

A female's lure light – a light-tipped rod sticking out from the top of her head – is perfectly suited for hunting in pitch-black waters. Light-producing bacteria in the rod flash pale blue and white, mimicking the appearance and motion of small ocean animals and attracting unsuspecting prey to her gaping mouth.

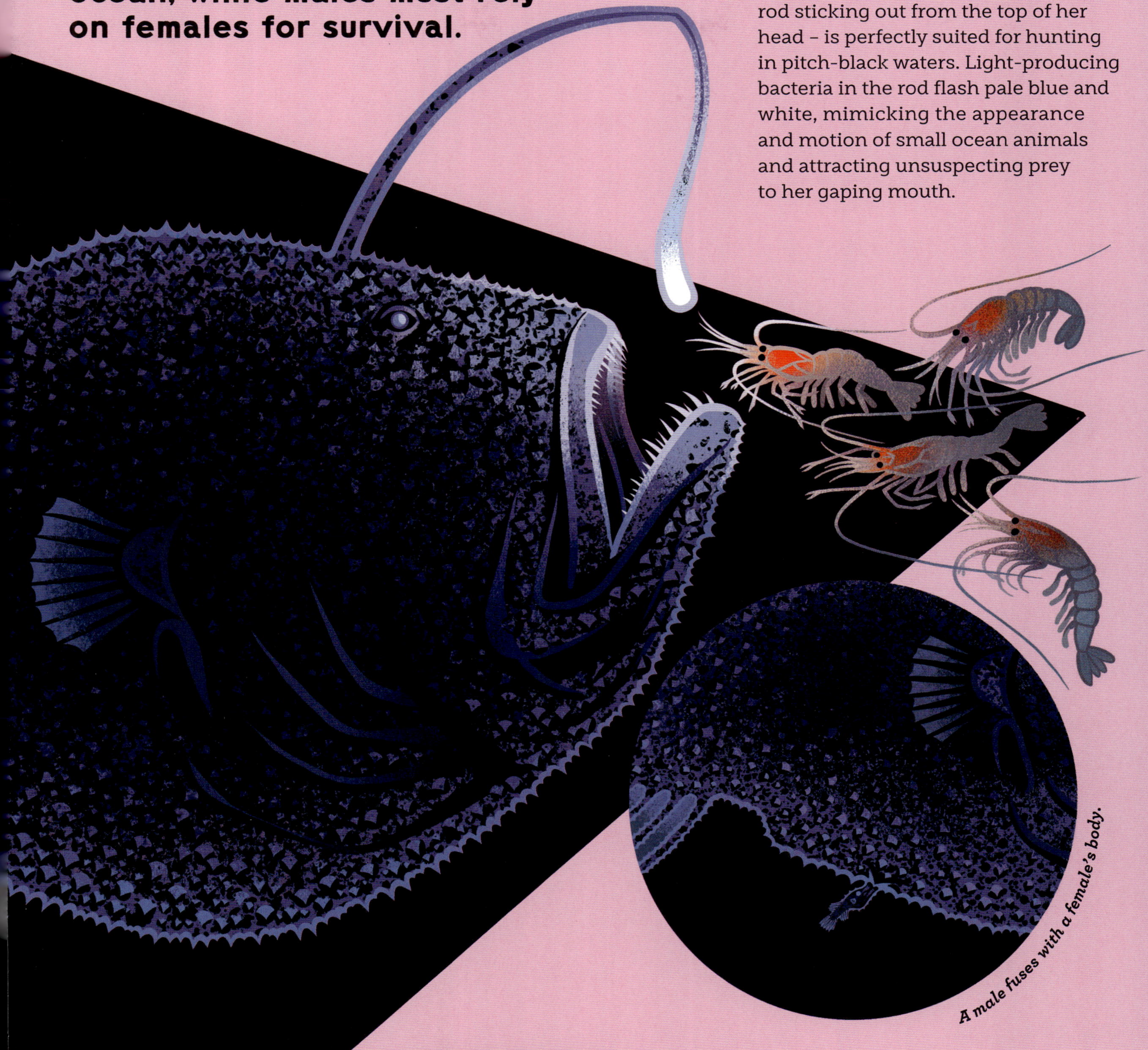

A male fuses with a female's body.

Strange but true

When a female encounters a tiny male, something extraordinary happens. He is so small that his best chance of survival is to stick to her, and that's what he does – literally. He fuses to her bottom and stays there for life, relying on her to feed him directly through her bloodstream and keep him alive. It's a strange arrangement, but she's big enough for both of them!

Self-cloning creatures

Cabbage aphid

She may be a minute sap-sucking insect, but the female cabbage aphid is also a survival star with a handful of mighty adaptive superpowers.

First of their kind

Female cabbage aphids typically give birth to around 60 to 100 daughters at the start of spring, via the biological process 'parthenogenesis' – the female-only ability to create offspring by yourself! Female aphids were the first species recognised to be capable of this seemingly magical power, nearly 300 years ago, in 1740.

Many female aphids are born with daughters and even granddaughters already developing inside them!

A wingless female with her young.

Billions of babies

Female cabbage aphids can make new aphids at a supercharged speed. Incredibly, when they're born, female cabbage aphids can already hold within themselves not only their daughters waiting to be born, but their *granddaughters* as well. This rare phenomenon, unique to females, is called the 'telescoping of generations'. It means female cabbage aphids can very, very quickly create multiple generations of all-female families. The awesome female founder of a population is called the 'fundatrix' or 'stem mother'. She can potentially have a billion descendants in a single season!

When a ladybird bites into an aphid's head, the aphid fights back by releasing deadly chemicals!

Small but mighty

Some female aphids have wings to escape predators, but wingless females deal with predators another way – by using powerful chemical weapons! Cabbage aphids enjoy broccoli, cabbage, Brussels sprouts and cauliflower, and wingless females store a useful chemical from these vegetables in their blood. When faced with a ladybird or another predator, they mix the chemical with a special compound in their body and fire off a deadly mustard oil bomb!

Although the female aphid firing the mustard oil weapon also dies afterwards, her brave sacrifice saves the rest of her colony and allows them to continue long after she is gone.

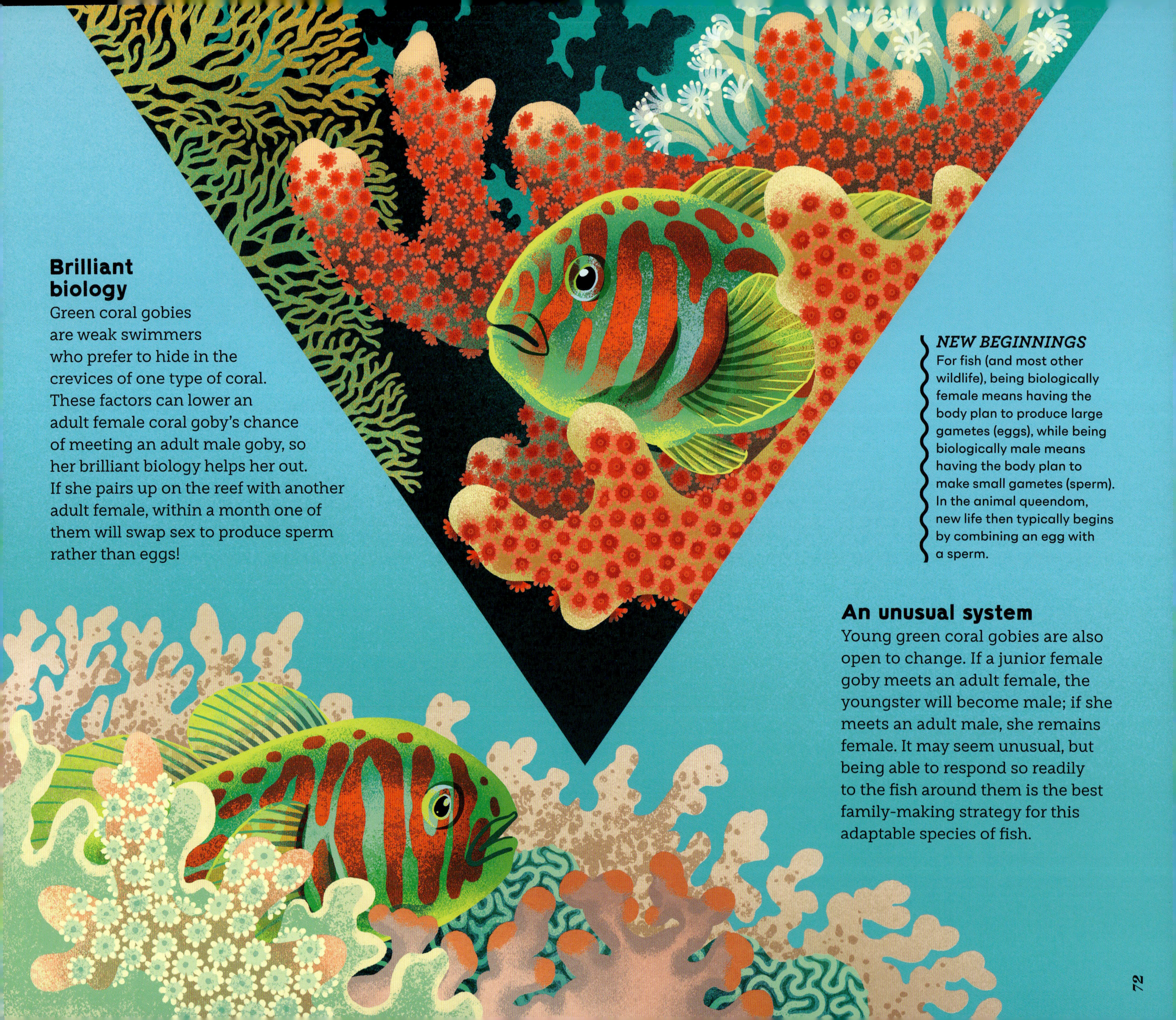

Brilliant biology

Green coral gobies are weak swimmers who prefer to hide in the crevices of one type of coral. These factors can lower an adult female coral goby's chance of meeting an adult male goby, so her brilliant biology helps her out. If she pairs up on the reef with another adult female, within a month one of them will swap sex to produce sperm rather than eggs!

NEW BEGINNINGS

For fish (and most other wildlife), being biologically female means having the body plan to produce large gametes (eggs), while being biologically male means having the body plan to make small gametes (sperm). In the animal queendom, new life then typically begins by combining an egg with a sperm.

An unusual system

Young green coral gobies are also open to change. If a junior female goby meets an adult female, the youngster will become male; if she meets an adult male, she remains female. It may seem unusual, but being able to respond so readily to the fish around them is the best family-making strategy for this adaptable species of fish.

Fantastically flexible fish

Green coral goby

For a tiny fish to thrive in a large, predator-filled ocean, flexibility is essential. Green coral gobies all start life as female but, with limited opportunities to find a partner and start a family, they have the rare ability to shift sex from female to male and back again!

A special species

For most species, the ability to produce either eggs or sperm is fixed: females cannot usually transform their bodies to become sperm-producing males, and males cannot usually change their bodies to become egg-producing females. However, the green coral goby can do both of those things – depending on who she meets!

Female coral gobies can change sex so that they and their partner can have babies.

Conclusion

We live in a vibrant and thrilling animal queendom, inhabited by exceptional females of all shapes, sizes and capabilities. In the pages of this book alone, you've been introduced to female animals who are fierce and fast, protective and powerful, sociable and smart. You've met record breakers and world-travellers, skilled leaders and cunning killers.

Each of them are complex, fascinating creatures that deserve to be celebrated, and they represent only a small selection of the world's amazing female wildlife!

The actions of brave, pioneering scientists – many of them women – have challenged old ways of thinking, and we now have a richer picture of female animals than ever before.

For the first time in history, females of different species are beginning to be considered and researched almost as much as male animals are. But there is a lot left to discover, and female animals are only starting to get the equal attention that they deserve.

The hope is for a future where we know as much about female animals as we do about males, and where our enhanced understanding leads to new discoveries about all of our incredible planet's wildlife.

Scientific knowledge is always growing and theories about our planet's animals are constantly changing. But for humans to understand the full story of life on Earth, we need scientists and researchers from all sorts of different backgrounds to contribute their ideas. That could include you – the reader of this book!

If you think nature is awesome and love to ask questions about the world around you, you could grow up to make the next big animal discovery! The more people care about and are curious about female animals, the more we will learn about wildlife in general, and the more we will be able to appreciate the true wonder of the incredible, inspiring **animal queendom**.

Female champions of the animal queendom

When curious and brave women finally got the chance to explore the natural world, a fuller and more accurate picture of female animals began to emerge. By pointing out where earlier male scientists had underestimated, misrepresented or simply ignored female animals, these trailblazing women forever changed how we understand the animal queendom.

1679
Maria Sibylla Merian shocked her 17th-century peers with her discovery that insects did not 'magically' appear, showing that silkworms emerged from eggs laid by female silkworm moths.

1976
Dr Katherine Ralls showed that many female mammals are larger than males, and highlighted the female blue whale (pages 54–55) as the most massive animal ever! Sadly, many initially overlooked her research. It wasn't recognised fully until 2024, when Dr Kaia Tombak's work proved Dr Ralls was correct.

1977
Professor Sarah Blaffer Hrdy's study of langur monkeys focused equally on females and males. It highlighted female animals as powerful strategists and challenged assumptions that animal mums are always nurturing.

1983
Professor Patricia Adair Gowaty uncovered the aggressive nature of female eastern bluebirds and how they take charge when seeking out mates. It is now accepted that most female animals have multiple mates and that female violence is not uncommon.

1996
Professor Naomi Langmore's research disproved older theories that female songbirds were silent, and woke the world up to the fact that most can sing!

1875
Antoinette Brown Blackwell bravely highlighted that scientist Charles Darwin's writing ignored female characteristics and presumed that females couldn't be fierce and feisty. Her work encouraged people to challenge assumptions about female animals.

1894
Eliza Gamble questioned Darwin's belief that female animals were usually smaller than males of the same species. She highlighted data in his research that showed the exact opposite! Her insights on size would inspire future scientists.

1966
Dr Alison Jolly's work with ring-tailed lemurs (pages 50–51) was the first to show that female primates can rule the roost by holding the top-ranking position in their group.

1974
Professor Jeanne Altmann put female animals in the spotlight, forever changing how animal data is collected. She revealed that earlier scientists had mostly ignored everyday female behaviour.

2013
Professor Daphne Fairbairn revealed that females are usually larger when female and male animals in a species differ in size. This is true in 86 per cent of animal classes (animal groups with shared characteristics – for example, mammals).

2025
Ambika Kamath and Melina Packer explored how human biases affect how animals are studied, particularly female animals. Their work – and the work of other brilliant women – is helping us discover more about the animal queendom!

Glossary

ADAPTATION A change in physical biology or behaviour that helps an organism to exist in a specific environment.

AGGRESSIVE MIMICRY When an animal is able to use the fact that they look like another animal or plant to trick their prey.

ALPHA The powerful leader of a group of animals, who often gets first choice of resources such as food or shelter.

BACTERIA Tiny, single-cell organisms that exist all around us.

BIAS An unfair preference for an idea, person or group that makes it difficult to see things clearly.

BLUBBER A thick layer of fat that lies under the skin of marine mammals such as whales and can store energy.

BREASTBONE A large, flat bone that sits in the centre of some animals' chests (e.g. birds).

CAMOUFLAGE Physical features that allow an animal to blend in with their surroundings to avoid detection.

CANOPY A layer of trees and other plants that act as a roof-like area over a rainforest.

CARCASS The body of a dead animal.

CARNIVORE An animal that gets its energy from eating other animals.

CARTILAGE Strong flexible tissue that forms parts of some animals' bodies (e.g. the discs in an African clawed frog's voice box).

CELLS The basic building blocks of every living thing.

CHROMATOPHORES Special cells that contain pigment and can produce colour.

COLONY A large group of animals of the same species that live together (e.g. ants).

DECOY Something that can be used to trick an animal or distract it from its goal.

DROUGHT A period of time when there is hardly any rain and the ground becomes dry.

ECHOLOCATION An ability that allows some animals (e.g. bats) to 'see' their surroundings in the dark by using sound waves to work out where objects are.

EMBRYO The name given to the developing form of an animal before it is ready to hatch or be born.

FACULTATIVE PARTHENOGENESIS The extremely rare ability for a female animal to have babies either with or without the input of a male.

FLUKES The two flat sections at the end of a dolphin, porpoise or whale's tailfin.

FORAGE The process of an animal searching for food in the area around them.

FREQUENCY The rate at which sound waves vibrate. Low frequency sounds vibrate slower and so sound lower in pitch, while high frequency sounds vibrate faster and so sound higher in pitch.

FUNDATRIX A wingless female aphid who is the founder of a population of potentially a billion aphid descendants in a single season.

FUNGI A type of organism that produces spores and is completely different from plants and animals.

GAMETE Special cells produced by female and male animals that are usually both required to create a baby animal. Gametes produced by female animals are called eggs and gametes produced by male animals are called sperm.

HEAT-BALLING A defensive tactic where a group of female bees work together to vibrate their flight muscles and create heat that can kill an attacking hornet.

KRILL Small crustaceans that can be found in all of the world's oceans and that are often eaten by larger sea creatures.

LARYNX Commonly called the 'voice box', this organ helps animals to produce sound.

LURE LIGHT An organ present in animals such as female anglerfish that allows them to attract prey towards their mouth.

MAGNETORECEPTION A sensing ability that allows an animal to detect the Earth's magnetic field – the invisible lines that run from the North to South pole.

MAMMAL Animals with backbones that produce milk and are warm-blooded.

MANDIBLES A pair of jawbones present in some animals. Mantises use their mandibles to bite and slice through prey.

MARSUPIAL A group of animals that give birth to young and then raise them in an external pouch on their bodies.

MARSUPIUM The pouch found in marsupials such as kangaroos, wallabies and koalas.

MATRIARCH Female leaders who are often older and more experienced members of a group of animals.

MOB CALLS Sounds made by birds in order to gather help when launching an attack.

NUTRIENTS Substances that give animals the energy that they need to grow, heal and stay healthy.

OCELLI Spots on an animal that look like eyes.

ORGAN A part of an animal's body with an important, specific job (e.g. heart, lungs).

PARALYSE To cause an animal to lose the ability to move.

PARASITE An organism that depends on another living thing for survival, often negatively affecting the thing it is relying on.

PARTHENOGENESIS The rare ability for a female animal to have a baby by themselves, without the input of a male.

PHONIC LIPS Folds of tissue that sit below a dolphin, porpoise or toothed whale's blowhole and allow them to produce sound underwater.

PIGMENT A substance that gives something colour.

PREDATOR An animal that hunts and eats other animals.

PREY An animal that is hunted by other animals.

REGURGITATE To bring food back up from the stomach and into the mouth.

REPUTATION What a large group of people think something or someone is like. Reputations can be negative or positive and may not always be accurate.

SAP A liquid that can help carry minerals, water and nutrients around the inside of a plant.

SCAVENGER An animal that prefers to feed on dead animals or plants rather than hunting live prey.

SEMI-RETRACTABLE A part of an animal that can be partially, but not fully, pulled back into its body.

SILK-FLICKING A skill found in some spiders, including female black widow spiders, where they can shoot out strands of silk from their spinnerets.

SLIPSTREAM The current created by a large whale as it swims along.

SOUNDWAVE Invisible energy created by vibrations that can be detected by some animals' ears.

SPINNERETS Organs found in spiders that allow them to spin silk to build webs and trap prey.

STATUS The social position of one animal in relation to another animal. The higher an animal's status, the more access to resources they tend to have.

STOOP The fast, steep dive that a peregrine falcon performs when hunting prey.

SUFFOCATE To be unable to breathe due to a lack of air.

TELESCOPING OF GENERATIONS A phenomenon where a female wingless aphid can have her daughters and granddaughters developing inside her at the same time.

TERMITE A small insect that lives in large colonies and eats fibres found in plants and trees.

TERRITORY An area of land that an animal or group of animals claim and work to keep as their own.

THERMOCEPTION A sense that allows some animals to detect differences in temperature.

TOXIN A poisonous substance produced by living organisms.

TRACTION The ability to grip the ground without slipping.

VENOM Poisons that are injected into animals through fangs, teeth or other sharp body parts.

VERTEBRATE An animal with a backbone.

WAGGLE DANCE Movements made by female worker honeybees that signal the location of pollen and nectar.

WINGSPAN The distance from the tip of one wing to the tip of the other wing in animals such as insects or birds.

Index